Aunt Pat's War

by June Nelson

Copyright © 2023 by June Nelson

All rights reserved.

The content contained within this book may not be reproduced, duplicated or transmitted without direct written permission from the author or the publisher.

Table of Contents

Introduction: Why I chose to write *Aunt Pat's War* 5
Chapter 1: Paris Memories – 1970 7
Chapter 2: Paris Resistance Reality – Bill's Story 10
Chapter 3: A Brief Sojourn with Fitz 15
Chapter 4: Time to Leave Paris 20
Chapter 5: Like Clockwork 23
Chapter 6: A New Life 26
Chapter 7: The Journey to London 32
Chapter 8: Harrods 37
Chapter 9: Leaving London 40
Chapter 10: Meeting Madame Basquille 43
Chapter 11: The Autograph Book 47
Chapter 12: Foreign Christmas 56
Chapter 13: First World War, Langerbrugge, 1914 58
Chapter 14: Switzerland 1914 62
Chapter 15: Swiss Life 65
Chapter 16: In Love 69
Chapter 17: Geneva and Education, 1916 73
Chapter 18: Fewer Words Mean More 77
Chapter 19: Culture and Freedom 81

Chapter 20: For the Best 85

Chapter 21: Dancing Shoes 89

Chapter 22: Time to Move On 92

Chapter 23: Villiers-sur-Mer 96

Chapter 24: Villa Durenne to Paris 99

Chapter 25: Guests at Villa Durenne 103

Chapter 26: Kitty, One of Life's Blessed 106

Chapter 27: Romance in France but Famine in Ireland 108

Chapter 28: A Proposal 111

Chapter 29: Destination Paris 115

Chapter 30: The Wedding 120

Chapter 31: Free and in Love 123

Chapter 32: Paris 1940 127

Chapter 33: A Brief Marriage 130

Chapter 34: Paris Is Liberated, 25 August 1944 134

Chapter 35: Those Who Were Lost 138

Chapter 36: Many Memories, Not Enough Time 142

Chapter 37: Crossing the Date off the Calendar 146

Epilogue: The Grave in Killeshin 149

June Nelson

Introduction

Why I chose to write Aunt Pat's War

Telling a good story is an art that I have always loved. Since I was very young, I have been enthralled listening to various people—mostly family members—telling stories about the people who have gone before them. I remember all the tales. Social history is fascinating. For one thing, it explains how we came to be. For another, it shows the development of lives influenced by family events as well as worldwide happenings. Births, marriages, deaths—each to some extent dictated, or at least influenced, by the vagaries of life's experiences.

I started my research by spending many lovely hours chatting to my Aunt Eileen in England and recording all the information and stories she had to tell about my family and especially Aunt Pat. She and her daughter, Christine, gave me endless support, for which I am so grateful. I spoke to my father about his memories of his aunt. It turned out that my parents spent their honeymoon in Paris with Pat in 1955. I rang my cousins in Co Laois and gathered some of their recollections. My father shared many amazing photographs and newspaper cuttings with me, which were invaluable. My cousin Adienne also gave me some wonderful old photographs, which I treasure. I researched each era, finding out as much as possible about how world events had affected Pat's life. Studying photographs and old newsreels proved extremely informative, as did digging up information on places where she had stayed and lived. I immersed myself in the music of the time, pored over everything I could find on the fashions, and chased down anything else that might have influenced her world or life.

Everything I discovered only reinforced my impression that Pat was a truly extraordinary woman, born before women possessed the right to vote. I felt privileged to be writing about such an intelligent woman, to know that our shared ancestors lived and died in India, that her mother—my great-great-grandmother—was born in India and died giving birth to her; that as a baby, she and her brother, John, were brought back to Ireland by two Hindu nurses with a goat, and that I own the gold Chaemseh Hand of God charm that accompanied the infant on that journey so long ago.

I met Aunt Pat on several occasions. Even as a child, I was fascinated by her, and I remember always feeling proud of her. *Aunt Pat's War* is a tale worth telling. It has taught me many things and massively influenced my own journey of personal development. Among the things Pat taught me: It's okay to speak out. It's okay to be brave. And most of all, it's okay to be a strong girl.

Thank you, Aunt Pat, for everything.

Chapter 1

Paris Memories – 1970

Pat's daydream in her flat on Rue des Acacias was interrupted by a sharp buzzer. She was feeling very nostalgic. Kitty, Pat's youngest sister, had just died, and she was constantly thinking about her. Pat's niece Eileen had come over to Paris for Kitty's funeral, and she would visit Pat that afternoon to chat with her, recording her memories with a view to writing a memoir. Ever since asking her, Pat had thought about nothing else. After the funeral service the previous afternoon, she had sat in a chair by the tall French window, listening to the blind accordion player on the street corner. Pat was totally oblivious to the changing, dusky light outside and the slight chill that came in through billowing lace curtains. She had no idea how long she had sat there. So many years went by in a kaleidoscope of images—her beginnings in Co Laois, at school in Belgium, then college in Switzerland, several journeys home, family births, marriages and deaths, her sister Kitty's arrival and subsequent marriage in France to Andre, Andre's murder by the communists, and the war years. The images sparked emotions Pat had long forgotten, particularly when she thought about all the goodbyes she had said throughout her life to many people she loved, knowing it was for the best. Recalling those times was a tough exercise for her, but she knew that if she were to tell her story, there were many painful memories that she could not leave out.

Pat welcomed Eileen into the flat, then proceeded to the kitchenette to boil the kettle. She forgot her apprehensions as the two started to chat about news from Co Laois. Not until they had eaten the fruitcake and enjoyed numerous cups of tea did Eileen take out her notebook and pen and ask Pat to talk about the first thing that came into her head. As was usual with Pat, she had decided to deal with the most difficult experience first—Bill, the Irish airman that she had hidden in her apartment during the war. Getting up from the table, she made her way over to her small bookshelves. Among her treasures was a framed photograph of a sandy-haired young man. On the table in front of him was an opened tortoiseshell box; in his hand, he reverently cradled what had been inside it—a wooden shamrock. "This is Chris, Bill's beloved friend. Bill had hand-whittled that shamrock," she said. "He left it as a parting gift, and it was one of my dearest treasures, which I gave to Chris when he came to see me one day in 1946."

Eileen eyed her with compassion. Bill's name was well known to her as Pat had spoken often about him down through the years.

"When I saw the Nazis marching into Paris and that disgusting, creepy man with his little tuft of a moustache in June 1940, I knew that I would have to help get rid of them in any way possible. I'd heard whispers that the café that Jacque ran, where I had always met my friends, played a significant role in the Resistance. I decided to speak to Sister Bernarde, who knew everything that was worth knowing about the underground movement in Paris. I knew she would advise me on how to broach the subject with Jacque in the safest way possible. This conversation set me on my dangerous yet worthwhile journey with the Paris Resistance. I didn't really understand what I was getting myself into, but by God, I was determined to give it my all."

In minute detail, Pat recounted how she had helped to collect Bill the day he first arrived in Paris. How she had nearly been caught by the Nazis and how they nearly captured him again on the morning of his escape from Paris. Her face reflected the affection she had developed for Bill; her expressions were animated as she unfolded the story of their time together. Eileen had always known that Pat was fond of Bill but hadn't realised to what extent. Then a hiccup caught in Pat's throat. Eileen jumped up and put her arm around Pat as the tears rolled down her cheeks. Never had she seen any sign of weakness in her aunt except when she recalled Kitty discovering her brutally murdered husband, Andre. Nobody would ever have guessed that Pat had suffered so much.

Eileen made a pot of much needed tea and placed it on the table between them. This gave Pat time to recover, and after a while, she continued with the story of Bill. Rubbing the precious wooden shamrock between her thumb and forefinger, she spoke in a much lower tone. Around two weeks after she had last seen Bill disappearing on the back of the motorbike towards his escape route, Sister Bernarde had arrived unannounced at her flat. She had known immediately that this was not a happy visit. The nun's face looked too concerned and serious. Pat felt her anxiety building, and she sat down without even asking her why she had come.

Damn this bloody war, Sister Bernarde thought. How terrible to have to hurt her dear friend like this. She stumbled as she took the chair across from Pat and leaned forward to clasp Pat's cold hands in hers.

"Pat, it's Bill. He is dead. He was captured with Tio, his Resistance contact. They tried to run for it, but the bastards shot them both in the back."

"*Merde*," Pat had said, and she put her hands to her head and wept.

Eileen wanted to ask her to continue and also to tell her about the mysterious Chris and his connection with Bill, but retelling the story this far had exhausted her aunt. Eileen shut her notebook and insisted that Pat go to her room to take a nap. Pat had suffered with her nerves in recent years and needed help at times to control her anxiety. Eileen did not want her to suffer a relapse.

Chapter 2

Paris Resistance Reality – Bill's Story

Bill had never met a woman like Pat before. Ever since his plane crashed in northern France, he had been listening to various members of the local Resistance as they discussed the safest and best way to help him. One thing he knew for certain—his chances of reaching his home in England were far better if he could make it to Paris safely. He still worried about his co-pilot and dear friend Chris. Never a day went by that he didn't pray for him.

Day after gruelling day, Bill never knew when he would have to gather up as much energy as possible and swiftly move on. He had injured his leg badly in the crash, and without proper treatment, he was constantly tired and often weak. Sometimes the owner of a Resistance-friendly farm would allow him to lie hidden on the ground outside for as little as an hour. The Resistance rules were strict, but Bill knew they had to be to protect all the brave souls in the escape chain who were risking their lives simply by giving them food. After nearly two weeks, he came close to Paris. He felt elated, but soon the joy mixed with creeping terror as this was by far the most dangerous part of his journey. The Germans had fenced Paris and established checkpoints to control all movement in and out. Reaching their final safe house before Paris took two days longer than Bill and his team had expected. Word had reached them of the capture and execution of fellow Resistance fighters in a nearby town, and they could sometimes hear sporadic gunshots in the distance, which reinforced their slow, cautious pace.

By the time they finally reached the rendezvous, he was exhausted. The throbbing of his injured foot and leg caused him to continuously bite down hard on his bottom lip to stifle any sound he might involuntarily emit. He and two of the Resistance men had picked up bicycles in the last village. They had cycled for about an hour, which was excruciating for Bill but totally necessary, their way lit only by the light of the crescent moon. Watched by a scavenging fox, they had hidden the bicycles and now waited in a moss-covered gulley that ran alongside the riverbank, leading to the bridge where they were to meet an important Irish-French Resistance fighter called Fitz. When the men spoke about Fitz, it was with reverence, telling Bill how lucky he was that this was his Paris contact.

As 4:30 a.m. approached, they climbed stiffly up onto the road, running as quickly as possible before hiding under the shadowy cover of the bridge. Suddenly, in the distance, they could hear the rumbling of an approaching truck. The truck moved very slowly, dimming its lights as it approached them. Helped by one of the men, Bill hobbled forward. A brief nod of heads in the moonlight the only greeting. Strong hands gripped Bill under the arms, and he whooshed up through the open door of the vegetable-filled truck. He swung his bad leg up behind the front passenger seat, emitting a deep shout of pain as he did so. A sharp slap landed on his ear, and he heard the words, "Godfathers! Do you want us all to get caught, idiot?!" whispered forcefully by a woman with a strange mix of an Irish and British accents. She introduced herself to Bill as Fitz, or Pat, and ordered him to say nothing if they were stopped. Totally shocked as he had been expecting a strong Irishman, Bill realised that this petite, brusque woman with her short spikey red hair was the legend he had heard so much about. Fitz was a woman, and Bill knew with just one look at her face that she was a very determined and very tough woman. Even with Fitz leading him, he was still feeling worn out and terrified of heading into the centre of Paris, where he knew there were large numbers of occupying Nazis committing brutal atrocities. But this lasted only a very short time as Pat's sizzling air of authority quickly started to reassure him. Long before Charles de Gaulle addressed the people of the French Resistance from London on 18 June 1940, the women of the French Resistance had been spoken of with respect.

When they reached Paris, dawn was just breaking with a misty pink glow, and the city was beginning to come to life. Bill was lying lengthwise behind the driver; the passenger seats were covered in old vegetable sacks. It had taken all his self-control not to sneeze or cough when the dust from the old cloth reached his nose and mouth. They had a number of routes they used, depending on the weather and most recent reports of Nazi activity. As they drove through the streets of Paris on their way to 8 Villa Guizot, Rue de Acacias, the shopkeepers were just rolling up their shutters.

They dropped off the goods to their usual Resistance-friendly shopkeeper. The banter, which Bill did not fully comprehend, seemed very jovial and relaxed. He kept his eyes down, and at times, upon hearing the tapping of steel-toed boots approaching, he would catch just a glimpse of the Nazi soldiers marching by on the footpath. He held his breath until he thought his head would burst and released it only when he could take no more. Thankfully they arrived at Pat's apartment without incident. The relief was intense all around.

Bill remembered nothing more about his arrival at Fitz' (or Pat's) flat apart from climbing so many steps that he thought his legs would give in. Like many of the airmen Pat would harbour during the war, Bill was suffering from total physical exhaustion and mental strain. She always kept the flat cool, with the shutters closed; the dim light allowed these men to feel more relaxed when they first arrived. She made sure she had a large bar of Lifebuoy soap, a clean facecloth, and a bowl of steaming water waiting for her guests along with a change of clothes when they eventually awoke from their much-needed sleep. Sometimes these men would have only a couple of hours before they were moved on. They always needed to be fully ready in case a quick departure was required. Quite often, Pat had to dress wounds using just TCP antiseptic and bandages made from old sheets. Bill was relieved to have his filthy woollen socks removed, even though it was painful beyond belief. Pat dressed his infected toe, and he hobbled to the table by the now opened windows. In a small curtained-off area in the living room, he could see her cooking something on a two-ringed cooker. As he waited, a shaft of sunlight warmed his injured foot on the herringbone parquet floor. The aroma of home cooking wafted over to where he sat, and soon, they were enjoying a bowl of stew with bread. Once their hunger was sated, Pat spoke. "I am glad you like my vegetable stew—luckily, I was able to keep some of the produce from the truck this morning." The 350 grams of rationed bread divided between them and washed down with a precious glass of red wine each was beyond satisfying.

Quickly gathering the dishes, Pat told Bill to sit in one of the two easy chairs beside a table with black wrought-iron legs and a foot pedal and a Singer sewing machine. The walnut tabletop concealing the sewing machine beneath it was covered by a small, square-shaped linen cloth embroidered with a crinoline-clad lady holding a parasol. These airmen were so exhausted from their journey and stress that Pat knew she could just chat away without interruption. She told him all about her life in Paris under the Nazis and the Resistance plan to get him over the Spanish border to Portugal.

In her clipped accent, she described the sheer terror on 14 June 1940 as 40,000 stormtroopers in their oppressive uniforms and dehumanising helmets marched into Paris, the front lines led by the beating of the Nazi drummers. Black horses with mounted soldiers towered above the Parisians. The Panzer IV tanks had rolled along behind, the stench of their engine fuel hanging in the air for a long time after they moved on.

Pat became so animated with her rage against the Nazis that she failed to notice that Bill was fast asleep. On and on she ranted. She described through gritted teeth how she had witnessed Hitler touring Paris on 23 June 1940, accompanied by Albert Speer, his favourite architect. She told the sleeping Bill that Hitler had guided his esteemed architect around the monuments of Paris as if he had created them himself. It was only when Bill let out a deep snore that Pat finally realised he was out cold. Leaving him there, she headed to bed, suddenly noticing how tired she was.

Chapter 3

A Brief Sojourn with Fitz

Hitler seemed to be at the peak of his narcissistic reign. Moving Napoleon's sons' remains alongside their father's tomb was symbolic. Only someone with great authority could do such a thing, and Hitler took great delight in lording it over the horrified Paris officials. German troops were posted at the entrance to most streets and roads into the city with shoot-to-kill orders, which made it even more difficult to transport stranded allied airmen.

Two days after Bill's arrival, Pat was up early. After washing at the sink in the little kitchenette, she daubed eau de cologne behind her ears and on her wrists. Taking her small packed lunch, she headed out the door to work. Keeping up established routines was very important for all members of the Resistance in Paris. She met her friend Patrice at the same place every morning, and together, they would head for a new venue that was whispered to them by the newspaper seller at the top of the street. There they sought supplies and information. That particular Friday morning, Pat hoped to get whatever rations were available but also to find out what arrangements had been made to move Bill out of Paris.

It did not take her long to realise the depth of Bill's love for his co-pilot, Chris. She had immediately taken to Bill and was very sympathetic to his need to determine Chris' whereabouts. She had seen too many broken hearts recently—particularly that of her poor sister Kitty. She had promised to ask about Chris and had written a small, encrypted note, which she attached to the back of one of her ration tickets. This was a tricky move, but it was the only way information could be passed to whomever needed it. She and Bill had spoken late into the night before. He told her he was from Wicklow town. At first, he had said very little about his life at home before he left Ireland to join the English air force. His dark black hair and deep blue eyes reminded her of her family in Ireland, and it was as if she had known him all her life. Obviously, he felt the same easy familiarity with Pat, and so he confided in her a secret about why he had left Ireland. Sitting at the table with all the lights out and blackout blinds drawn, lit only by a single candle which cast dancing shadows as he raised his hands, first in despair and then in anger, he told a story he had never imagined he would tell—especially not to someone he had just met.

Pat watched as he closed his eyes to speak. She was afraid to move in case she might disturb him. The roar of bombs dropping in the distance seemed to fade as her mind processed the images his words portrayed. Bill's father, Jack, was a dock working on the quay at Wicklow Harbour. He was a tall, wide-shouldered man who spoke very little, working hard every hour he could to support his wife and five children. Bill's mother's name was Blatheann, "flower" in Gaelic, and it was her name and beauty that had attracted Jack to her. Together they had three handsome boys and two beautiful girls. Bill was the mother's favourite, and his younger sister Sinead the father's. Life was tough living in the two-room cottage near the harbour, but they were happy. It was a house filled with laughter and contentment even though they hadn't much money. Bill spoke so quickly and quietly that it took all Pat's concentration to take in the horror he described.

It all started when his mother's brother, Sam, came to stay. The atmosphere in the house had changed immediately, especially as Sam started to come in drunk every evening after playing cards with some of the local dockers. One evening, while the family were in their uncle's house close by, Sinead was at home by herself, just waiting for the bread to finish baking before joining her family, when Sam came in. Although Sinead was fourteen, two years younger than Bill, she was very childish in her ways. Being Jack's pet and the youngest, she was doted upon by all. A beautiful, dark-haired girl with a dimple in the middle of her chin—what a picture she made, lifting a tendril of dark curls from her face as she wrapped the hot, oven-fresh bread in a tea towel.

The bread lying on the kitchen floor first made Bill aware that something was wrong. He stooped to pick it up when an animal groan made him lurch towards his parents' bedroom door. For a second, he stood transfixed at the sight of his uncle's bare bottom rising up from between the skinny white legs of poor, innocent Sinead. Her head was tilted back, and he would never forget the look of terror and pain in her beautiful dark eyes. Blind rage took hold of Bill, and the next thing he remembered was his father and older brother pulling him off Sam's battered body.

Time had no meaning after that. Just remembered flashes of voices, either raised or whispering, mumbling. Now and then a face loomed into his vision, and suddenly he felt somebody shake him by the shoulders, crying out his name.

Tears were streaming down Bill's face, and Pat put both her hands over his, begging him to stop; he did not need to tell her anything more. But he insisted on finishing his life-changing story. He explained that his brother had immediately run to get the parish priest, and between them, they had dragged Sam's lifeless body into the back yard, where they covered it in an old cloth until they made a plan. Bill's mother had taken Sinead to an aunt's house. During the night, they buried Sam in a shallow grave behind the old quarry. They decided to get Bill away from Wicklow as fast as possible as they feared he would be unable to handle staying where the memories of Sinead's trauma would haunt him.

Damaged and shocked, Bill went to England until things calmed down at home. The parish priest gave him a letter for his colleague in London, where he knew Bill would get all the help he needed. A broken young man left for England that early morning; the sight of his father at the dockside was to be his last.

Neither Pat nor Bill slept well that night, but the following day, Pat knew it was imperative that she stay alert in order to see Bill safely on his way.

The tension in the ration queues was always high, but today Pat sensed that one of the boulangères *was* making an extra effort to connect with her. Deciding to take the risk, she passed him the ration ticket with the note attached. As the boulangère handed back her ration card and ration book, he attached the escape plan for Bill underneath it. Pat left quickly, chatting to Patrice as normal. She could hardly wait until she got home later that evening to read the note. She was told to meet her contact at Café Jacque that evening at eight p.m.

Once they had eaten dinner and put away the last of the dishes, Pat told Bill they were going to listen to the seven p.m. news on her radio. She was especially proud of this French-made Phillips Melodies A49A radio. Checking her watch repeatedly, she turned the dial, and after a brief time, the radio warmed up. Radio Londres came to life with the uplifting words, "Ici Londres! Les Français parlent aux Français!" ("This is London Calling! The French speaking to the French!"). Pierre Boudin, the programme commentator, led the coded messages that were hidden in every broadcast. Pat quickly jotted down some words on the notepad lying open on the side table and then quickly hid them behind the false skirting board in the kitchenette. What a vision Pat made, waiting to hear if de Gaulle would speak. The Free French had five minutes to broadcast each day, and every supporter listened with anticipation to hear if their leader would make a speech.

Bill stared at the petite Irish woman standing at attention in her black cigarette pants and white blouse, with a red turban on her head. He saw her put her hand on her heart as she listened intently to the commander of the Free French forces, General Charles de Gaulle. He watched in fascination afterwards while she sang along to Benjamin Clarke as he crooned "Les Amis du Maquis" in English, her posture straight, head high, her dramatic green eyes flashing. Bill felt he was in strong, safe hands.

Chapter 4

Time to Leave Paris

As Pat walked quickly towards Café Jacque that evening, she tried to keep her head down and not attract any unwanted attention, especially from the German soldiers posted at every street corner. Whenever someone addressed her, she replied with a smile and a nod. Her hands in their white cotton summer gloves felt the cold steel of her small handgun in her leather clutch. All around her was a furtive atmosphere; people seemed to move quickly to avoid the soldiers. Eyes watched everything and you never knew for what reason, whether they were friend or foe.

When she reached Café Jacque, the proprietor, Jacque, greeted her and led her to a table at the end of the window overlooking the street. The aroma of coffee hung in the warm air. The café was starting to take on its cosy evening glow as the light faded rapidly outside. An attractive waitress in a Breton tee-shirt and tight skirt was lighting thick, well-used candles on all the tables, which were covered with red and white checked tablecloths. The resident piano player had taken his seat and was gently tinkling tunes.

Pat sat where she had a clear view of everything going on in and outside the café. Jacque arrived with a small glass of absinthe and an ashtray, making direct eye contact with her. The folded newspaper was already on the table when she arrived, two pens lying beside it. She removed her gloves and put them into her handbag, then retrieved her cigarettes, lighter, and lipstick, taking care not to draw attention to the concealed pistol. Placing the distinctive lighter, with its green dragon emblem facing upwards, on the table, she touched up her deep red lipstick. Taking up the newspaper, she had a quick look at the crossword while sipping her drink.

Not long afterwards, a very tall, thin man arrived at the café. He saluted Jacque and took the seat in front of Pat, removing his light rain mac to reveal his black shirt and trousers and white priest's collar. So far, this carefully rehearsed plan was going smoothly, thought Pat. Father Brendan was a good friend of Sister Bernarde, and she had met him on numerous occasions. She and the priest chatted for a while. They spoke just loudly enough to be heard. He took out his own copy of the newspaper and then took off his wristwatch, leaving it on the table where they both could see it. Each taking up a pen, they started the same crossword in their respective papers for the allotted competition time. This had become a regular routine and caused much amusement in the café when tempers flared as dubious words and spellings were questioned.

When the door to the café burst open, Pat pushed her handbag farther under her seat with her foot to hide it from the three very drunk Nazi officers who entered and started shouting at Jacque, ordering wine. The atmosphere immediately became tense, and both Pat and Father Brendan knew they would have to be very careful. In the space between some of the genuine words, Father Brendan wrote code words, directing Pat towards the Resistance-planned drop-off point for Bill. Luckily for them, the German soldiers were more interested in the attractive barmaid, in particular the speed it took for her to produce more wine. Pat waited for some time, then, using the same coded method, she asked if Father Brendan had any news of Chris.

They discreetly swapped newspapers, and then it was time to leave. Walking home, Pat could not wait to see what route the Resistance had chosen to use for Bill's departure. She decided not to tell him that evening but would let him catch up on rest, as he would need it for the arduous journey ahead.

Chapter 5

Like Clockwork

Pat stole out of the flat early the following morning to visit Sister Bernarde and collect some fresh bread. She arrived at the convent at 8:15 a.m., having walked through Paris on a beautiful sun-kissed morning. All Pat could think about was the plan to get Bill out early on Sunday morning. She rang the little bell at the entrance. One of the novice nuns answered and brought her into the convent kitchen with its cream-coloured Aga and a coffee pot gurgling away on the hob. Bernarde, as Pat called her, was sitting at the long breakfast table, coffee cup in hand.

"Ah my dear friend, what a lovely early surprise," said the nun as she poured a steaming, pungent-smelling mug of coffee. *Such a treat to get real coffee*, thought Pat. This was not the first time they had worked together to help transport airmen home. They both knew they were taking a great risk, not just for themselves but for anyone connected to them, so they planned Sunday morning with great attention to detail. They needed to get Bill out of Paris as quickly as possible. This would take guts, well-coordinated changeover stops, and plenty of luck. The city was on high alert at present, and both Pat and Bernarde felt nervous when they said goodbye. The following twenty-four hours would be very tense.

When Pat arrived back at the flat, Bill was already up and sitting at the little table. She put on boiled eggs, and they sat down to breakfast.

Aunt Pat's War

As they drank their coffee made with roasted acorns, Pat finally told Bill he was to leave at 3:30 the following morning. Neither of them was under any illusion that it was going to be easy, but nevertheless, Bill was elated. Finally, a chance to get home and a chance to find out something about Chris.

The day passed slowly. They both needed to rest but found it very difficult as their nerves were stretched. Pat tried to hide hers with false bravado and insisted they eat dinner together and listen to Radio Londres. Lighting candles in the sitting room, they sat in perfect companionship until the deep silent night rolled in.

Up, alert, washed and dressed in minutes, with false papers and a parcel of food, Bill left 8 Rue de Acacias for the last time. Trying to keep up with Pat was especially difficult; although his leg was much better, his foot had not fully healed. He knew he had no choice but to grit his teeth and push on. The door to the convent was slightly ajar, and there they met with men from the local Resistance. Bernarde gave Bill a knapsack with some provisions he would need and a knife wrapped in a leather pouch. As she handed him an old tweed coat, she met his eyes and said, "Your friend Chris is safe. He has been interned by the Germans near where you crashed." Tears rolled down Bill's cheeks as he grabbed her hands, but Pat put an end to this emotional moment in the fear that he would not be able to keep it together if the Nazis stopped him.

"Merde, Bill. Everyone's life is in danger the longer we wait here." As she helped him up onto the same truck he had arrived in, she ordered him in her no-nonsense whisper, "If stopped, don't speak unless I nod at you, and just reply if spoken to directly, okay?" They went out through the gates of the convent with their delivery of vegetables as usual. It was 4:30 a.m. by then, and the streets were quiet as it was Sunday morning. Pat had read her tarot cards the previous evening and had foreseen no trouble.

Suddenly she sensed movement farther up the street they were travelling on and told the driver to turn into the little lane by the Catholic church and turn off the engine. Wide-eyed and holding their breath, the three of them stared ahead, too petrified to move as an early morning patrol marched by. One of their many Resistance contacts along the way had been observing their progress. He opened his door onto the street quickly and noisily as the soldiers passed, causing them to react; they looked to see where the noise was coming from, so they missed the silent lorry parked up the alley. As the truck reversed out slowly, nobody spoke or moved. The rest of the journey proved uneventful.

As they said goodbye, Pat took Bill's slightly shaky body and gave him a tight hug. They had pulled into a barn just off one of the main roads that led toward the south of France. Once there, the Resistance hoped they could make it over the mountains into Spain and then on to Portugal. Bill took Pat's hands in his and told her he would get some sign to her that he had made it. Tears rolled down his cheeks as he thanked her for all she had done for him.

A shrill whistle and a Peugeot Terrot 750cc GT motorbike roared towards them. Bill smiled at Pat and made the sign of the cross before he climbed onto the back of the bike, which drove off in a haze of petrol fumes, quickly disappearing into the distance.

Having no time to waste, Pat said goodbye to her Resistance companion. Abandoning the truck in the barn, they went their separate ways by bicycle. It took two solid hours of cycling for Pat to get home. Climbing the stairs, she thought she would pass out with exhaustion, and when she entered the empty flat, the silence suddenly struck her. She would miss Bill.

On her way to the kitchenette, she noticed a little hand-whittled, shamrock-shaped piece of wood on the sewing-machine table alongside a note from Bill. Bringing the hand-made gift into her bedroom, she placed it on her bookshelf with her other treasures. Bill was only one of many airmen that she would help repatriate during the course of the war—but he always remained her favourite.

Chapter 6

A New Life

As a child, Pat was always fascinated by the framed, coloured print of the Eiffel Tower that hung in the back parlour of the Glenside Pub, her Killeshin home. Pat's mother, Ellen, had placed it there in 1904 shortly after the family bought the pub. From time to time, Ellen took it down and dusted it with pride while she daydreamed about her exotic journey from India as a small baby. Ellen's mother had died in childbirth, and so her father, Patrick Colgan, decided that it would be best to send his two children home from India to be brought up in Co Laois.

The children pursued the long journey over land and sea, accompanied by two Indian nurses and a goat. Years later, Ellen bounced her own young daughter, Pat, on her knee as she sat for a well-earned rest and recounted every little detail she had been told about her early life. Young Pat—or Judith Winifred, as she was christened—was spellbound by her mother's depiction of India in all its colour and pageantry.

Pat's grandmother, Sarah, had married a man who served in the British army. Like other emigrants, they left Ireland full of optimism and hope, in this case on a long sea journey to India. Sarah became a nurse, working under Florence Nightingale while her husband, took part in the

Charge of the Light Brigade. It could be said that Pat's ancestors had the ideally combined genes to create the warrior of the Second World War that Pat became. On many a wet afternoon, Ellen and Pat took cloths, gingerly opened the china cabinet in the corner of the parlour, and lovingly dusted with great reverence the remnants of that past Indian life. The corner cabinet had three shelves. The first displayed a lovely photograph of Ellen and Michael's wedding. Ellen gazed with beautiful intelligent eyes from behind her veiled hat, while Michael's chest swelled with the pride he obviously felt when marrying the beautiful and well-heeled Ellen. As each of her children was born, Ellen placed a lock of their hair in little silver frames on either side of the wedding photograph. These frames were lightly dusted and handled with care, none more than little Vera's as she was a special child who required additional care. Ellen couldn't help but sigh deeply each time she touched Vera's framed keepsake. It had always been clear that Vera could not stay with the family, as her needs were simply too great.

The second shelf held Michael's pocket watch, which Ellen had given to him as a wedding gift. Alongside the watch was a cross-stitched keepsake of their wedding date and place.

The third shelf held the christening gifts given to the children by their godparents. Pat, being the eldest, received a silver tankard. As each child was born, his or her name was carved into the tankard along with the date of birth. Pat's mother had given her a hand-crafted golden Indian charm on a chain, since she was the first-born girl. The Indian nurses who travelled with Ellen and her elder brother John had given it to Ellen, as it had belonged to her mother, Sarah. Pat loved to admire and hold this special talisman, imagining the amazing journey the charm had been on. The dusting ritual was completed when everything was replaced in the cabinet and the key turned firmly in the lock to ensure that no accidents could happen to the precious contents.

As the years went by, Pat had many duties around the pub and homeplace. Ellen had chronic arthritis, which developed rapidly. With the birth of each child, she seemed to lose more and more ability to perform even the simplest of household tasks. Eventually, Pat had to help raise her younger sisters along with carrying out other daily chores, including washing potatoes at the freezing trough in the back scullery. She then carried the potatoes back into the kitchen, boiled them, and mashed them. When the potatoes were cold, she carried them out in a large metal bucket to feed the nuzzling pigs. It was a heavy and arduous task, but Pat really loved the animals, whose affection for her was obvious. The moment her dark head appeared with the feast, the pigs snorted and rubbed against the gate. For years, Pat created fond memories, spending time with these beloved creatures and choosing nicknames for them. She endured absolute torment as each one was led either to slaughter or market. Times were harsh and every penny mattered. Pat learned quickly to balance her emotions.

Ellen's brother, John Colgan, had married Ada Hayden from the nearby town of Castleroe. John had followed the family tradition by joining the British army, where he rose to the rank of major and took part in the first Boer War. He and his wife had a good lifestyle but were not blessed with children. They lived abroad and each time they came back to Ireland on holidays, they felt concern for the tough situation the Fitzpatricks faced, especially as Ellen's health continued to deteriorate. Once, while standing on a chair trying to put plates back up on the kitchen shelf, Ellen took a bad fall, permanently damaging her back. This made caring for poor little Vera even more of a handful; the child required constant attention and needed to be carried everywhere. On many occasions, John and his wife asked the Fitzpatricks to allow them to sponsor Pat and pay for her further education, but the Fitzpatricks wouldn't hear of it, particularly as Pat was such an energetic and important help—not to mention life force—in the home. As Christine, Patrick, Scholastica, Gertrude, John, Kitty, and Vera grew, Ellen relied upon Pat even more. Eventually, this began to affect the girl's schooling.

One day, as Michael was stocking the pub for the weekend customers, Mr Johnston, the local schoolmaster, arrived to speak to him. Mr Johnston indicated his deep concerns that Pat had been missing so much school, as she was highly intelligent. He suggested that if the rumour about the offer to sponsor Pat was correct, Michael should consider allowing his daughter to accept the offer to help with her education. That night, when the pub closed, Michael and Ellen sat beside the stove in the kitchen and whispered to each other tearfully. No matter how long they spent teasing out the alternatives, they both knew in their hearts that there could be only one solution—they would have to allow Pat to go with the Colgans. They would need to let John and his wife know as soon as possible to give them time to plan the best future for Pat. With slow, hesitant movements, Michael took down the walnut writing case and ink pen. As Ellen wept silently and Michael tried to clear the knot in his throat, they wrote the letter that was to change all of their lives forever.

After two weeks, the Colgans received the wonderful news. They loved eleven-year-old Pat and for some time had been secretly making plans to help educate her. By telegram, they informed Michael and Ellen that they had contacted a convent school in Langerbrugge, Belgium, which had been highly recommended by army friends and where they felt confident Pat would be accepted as a pupil. French nuns ran it and taught numerous subjects that would interest Pat. All of this was organised without Pat's knowledge. However, when the telegram arrived, Ellen and Michael knew they needed to break the news to her as soon as possible.

Ellen sent the other children out with their father. It was a beautiful early evening in May, a wonderful time of day when the sun chased strange shadows into dark corners of houses with low ceilings and beams. A patch of brown lino on the floor under the oak table looked warm and inviting. Pat lay down on her tummy, hands under her chin, crossing and uncrossing her bare ankles, daydreaming while gazing at the ornate china cabinet. Closing her eyes for a moment, she drifted into near sleep, aware of the beat of the clock on the mantlepiece. She felt content, as getting such time to herself was unusual. The parlour door closed gently, disturbing her reverie. Looking up, the girl saw her beloved mother walking with her usual stiffness towards the china cabinet.

"Ah, Pat, my dear one. I have something to speak to you about." Pulling herself to her feet, Pat stood and watched as her mother removed the gold Indian charm from the cabinet. "You know that your father and I love you deeply."

Ellen swayed suddenly, and Pat ran to help her. "Mother, what is wrong? Tell me! Can I help you?"

Ellen allowed her daughter to help her to one of the fireside chairs and lower her into it. Sitting up as straight as possible, she began to speak. Tears rolled down her cheeks, but she managed to tell Pat everything from the very beginning. When she finished, she took Pat's hands in hers and gently stroked them, placing the gold Indian hand charm in her daughter's open palms. "So, you see, my brave, clever pet, your father and I see such spirit in you that we know that it would be wrong for us to deny you this chance in life to use the gifts you were given. We made this decision out of love for you. We know you will make the very most of it."

Pat felt sick, her stomach turning into an iron knot. She stood up and was just about to shout out in anger when Ellen suddenly lay back against the chair like a deflated ragdoll. She held her arms out to Pat, who took one gentle lurch and tumbled into them, gulping down her tears.

From that evening on, the atmosphere in the Fitzpatrick household changed. Pat's younger sister, Christine, was just nine years old when Pat passed the torch over to her. Pat diligently trained and helped her little sister become accustomed to the chores she would have to take over when Pat left. They had always been very close. Christine was as capable as Pat but had a very different personality; whereas Pat was serious-minded and meticulous, Christine went about her chores with a smile, singing to herself, and she loved to play pranks on customers. Though Pat possessed a strong, stubborn streak, Christine could not have wished for a more loyal ally. Many a time, Pat covered up for Christine's jokes that had gone just a little too far—like the time Christine placed a live chicken in the outside toilet to frighten her father. He did not see the funny side of it as he slipped and fell on top of the poor bird, killing it instantly. Pat calmed her father's anger and cajoled him into seeing the incident as an innocent, childish prank. As usual, Pat was the peacemaker of the family. At night, as the girls lay side by side in the cosy bed above the kitchen, they whispered their thoughts to each other, vowing to remain as close as they were then, no matter what.

Chapter 7

The Journey to London

As John and Ada were based in Colchester at the time, they received the letter from Co Laois quite quickly. Once the school in Langerbrugge confirmed Pat's place, they sent a telegram by return, letting Michael and Ellen know that Pat should be ready to travel by 14 June. A few days later, a large parcel was delivered to Killeshin, causing great excitement. The parcel contained a lovely leather suitcase for Pat. When she opened it, she found two envelopes, one of which held her itinerary and travel documents, and the other was a letter saying how delighted they were for her. From that day onwards, Pat's imminent departure never left her thoughts, alongside feelings of apprehension and excitement.

As the date drew closer, Pat felt troubled, not least by thoughts of leaving her family and home. During restless nights, she lay awake thinking what she might do. *If I speak now and say I just can't go, I could stay home in Killeshin. Uncle John would forgive me eventually. Sure, couldn't I go with them another time? Yes, that's it. I would be older then, more capable. Mother wouldn't need me as much, and Christine would be more mature and capable of taking over from me. They need me, they really do.*

Whenever she attempted to open her mouth to express these thoughts, though, a little voice from the back of her mind stopped her.

The only thing that kept Pat from breaking down the day before her departure was Ellen's promise of spending time alone with her two eldest girls that afternoon. It was the type of warm June day that only early summer can conjure, with bright blue skies and wispy white clouds gliding peacefully in the warm breeze. Pat and Christine linked their mother's frail arms as they slowly climbed up Killeshin Hill to the church grounds. Holding hands, they sat on Ellen's shawl, covering the well-tended grass in the sunshine. Only the sound of the curlews interrupted the comforting whispers of the trees. Looking out across the lush land, Ellen spoke, "Remember, Pat, this is your home. We are here for you, always." Christine hugged her mother and Pat tightly, and then they sat in utter silence until teatime beckoned.

The evening before Pat's departure was a difficult one. The younger children did not really understand what was going on but had a sense that something was different. They all ate their tea together. Even though Pat's favourite food had been cooked with love for her, she had no appetite. They were then allowed into the good parlour, which was usually reserved for Christmas, funerals, or the priest's visits. As a special treat, they shared a large fruitcake for the occasion, and each child received a piece with a glass of lemonade. When the cake was gone, Michael stood at the fireplace, and after clearing his throat, he told the family to raise their glasses to Pat. They took their places for the evening rosary; the murmuring of the prayers droned on, and Pat looked out through the open wooden slats of the dining chair she knelt against and wondered when she would ever hear this sound again. Once they'd said the Memorare, they all sang the popular Count John McCormack song "Macushla" together. As Michael finished the last verse, the mood in the room turned very sombre and silent. Noticing the strain on everyone's face, Ellen insisted they all go up to bed. She did not want Pat's last evening to become too emotional.

On 14 June, they awoke Pat at four a.m. As she was still very sleepy, Ellen helped her to get dressed. By lamplight, Pat, Ellen, and Michael strode to the postal lorry, where Paddy, the driver, waited to bring Pat to the boat in Dublin. They all knew Paddy very well, which helped to put Ellen and Michael's worries to rest. While he was loading the luggage into the back of the lorry, Michael took Pat's little hand in his and placed Ellen's on top. The three squeezed and hugged each other tightly, recognising a moment of no return.

Paddy opened the passenger door for Pat to climb in—he was in a hurry to leave as the stricken faces were too much for him to bear. The girl sat up very straight in the passenger seat, her stomach churning as he tucked a woollen blanket around her shivering body. Trying not to cry, Pat peeked out at her parents and gave them a brief wave goodbye. Christine's white face peering from the bedroom window was the last image of home that Pat would see for a long time. She could no longer hold onto her tears, which flowed down her face. They stopped only when she fell asleep.

Arriving at the harbour in Dún Laoghaire was daunting. The cold, salty air and screeching gulls were all new to Pat. It was about midday, and the place was heaving with people. Everyone seemed to be in a hurry, dealing with either families or officials or carrying luggage. Paddy, a very kind man and himself a father, had brought many a saddened passenger to board this very boat, and he took great care of Pat. Once they had presented the ticket to the purser, he immediately beckoned to an elderly nun who was travelling on the same ship. Her name was Sister Gerard, and she was a cousin of Paddy's. By chance, he had found out she would be travelling on the same boat and knew she would look out for Pat.

Soon Pat and Sister Gerard and the rest of passengers boarded the boat and received directions to their cabins.

Pat and Sister Gerard had been allocated two of the bunks in the same three-bunk cabin. Left alone to arrange her night clothes, Pat began to notice the silence. She was so used to the constant chattering of her little brothers and sisters that she had never really thought about how it would be if they were not around. Suddenly she felt very alone and frightened; as Sister Gerard started to put away Pat's small bag, the girl could not control a deep sob. "Oh, my poor child, they have expected too much of you," the nun said. She tried to console her young companion by rubbing her arm until Pat withdrew and clambered up to the top bunk to take a nap.

Waking just as they pulled out into the Irish Sea, Pat felt the surge of the water roll the boat. She jolted up quickly, asking Sister Gerard if they could go on deck for their last view of Ireland. They got ready, and up they went. The deck was crowded with all types of people, some travelling for work, some for pleasure, and some taking the first stage in an even longer journey. There was a common feeling that everyone was soaking up all the elements of their leave-taking. The smell of the briny air, the sound of the squealing gulls scavenging for food, the sight of the ever-shrinking harbour and behind it the Sugarloaf Mountains bathed in afternoon light, all accompanied by the murmur of people in expectation of change.

The purser, whom Paddy had handsomely tipped, came strolling down the deck. Seeing the serious faces of Pat and Sister Gerard, he started chatting away about what to look out for on the journey ahead. Pat began to relax as the friendly purser, whose name was Des, distracted her from her departure. After they had walked around the boat and taken in every detail of the view, Des took his leave, wishing Pat and Sister Gerard a good afternoon as they went below deck again. Unfortunately, taking a wrong turn, they ended up in the steerage section. Families all tumbled together with bags at their feet; children were running around, shouting and being yelled at. Babies cried and red-faced women tried to keep them calm. Men sat around smoking pipes, playing card games, or spectating. Clothes were dull, and in many cases, people wore numerous layers curled round their bodies to save having to carry too much. The air was pungent with body sweat, tobacco, and soiled nappies. Sister Gerard quickly guided them to a stairwell, and they eventually arrived at their cabin. Pat felt a wave of relief wash over her. She was grateful for the quiet and privacy of her three-bunk cabin and that Uncle John and Aunt Ada had organised everything so well.

This detour through steerage made an impression on her that was to serve her well as she experienced many changes in the days to come.

The boat arrived in Holyhead late morning. There was no time to spare as Pat scrambled to collect her luggage and dashed to catch a train to London. She knew that Aunt Ada planned to do a lot of shopping there. The arrangements had been made with the store to send Pat's school clothes ahead to Langerbrugge. Waving a quick goodbye to Sister Gerard and thanking her yet again, Pat followed Des, who carried her luggage to a cab. Soon, she was on the train to London where Aunt Ada would meet her.

The screech of the train pulling into Paddington deafened her. When the engine let out a large whoosh of black smoke and the siren sounded, she thought her heart would stop. She held her breath as the steam evaporated. Pat was relieved to see her beloved Aunt Ada standing there. All was well.

London was pulsating with noise, lights, and smells that Pat loved from the outset. The Colgans had kept the biggest treat a secret from her until they arrived at the gates of the small cottages attached to the Tower of London. Uncle John and his family were entitled to stay here because of his army service in India. Ada took great delight in seeing Pat's look of wide-eyed disbelief. The girl could not take in the fact that she was going to sleep so close to where a royal wife of Henry the Eighth was beheaded. As soon as they could, they left their bags in the cottage and walked the short distance to the Connaught Hotel, where they treated themselves to a delicious tea.

Chapter 8

Harrods

The Tower of London looked dauntingly sinister the following morning, surrounded by the grey-blue mist rising from the Thames. Ada and Pat got up, dressed, and took a step outside to gaze at the amazing sight. The service maid slowly cut the loaf of crusty bread bought an hour earlier, paying attention to each slice. Sitting down to a strong pot of tea, the two of them ate bread, butter, and jam and gulped back tea, giddy with the excitement of the trip into the London shops that lay ahead for them. As they finished their breakfast, Aunt Ada told Pat that the folder and large manila envelope on the table held the list of items she would need for her new school. For the first time, Pat caught a glimpse of what was in store—a photograph of the school, its extensive grounds, the nearby village of Langerbrugge, and the larger city of Ghent. She glanced at the list of subjects, some of which she had never heard of. She was filled with concern and looked to her aunt. Ada closed the folder and told her not to worry, that everything would work out in good time. As she sat silently beside Ada, Pat briefly forgot about the life she had left behind in Killeshin.

London was so busy that it took ages for the cabbie to find a suitable place to stop and let the two off. The doorman at Harrods held the door for them, and they headed for the children's section. They asked for the school uniform department, and a saleswoman led them into a department displaying many institutions' uniforms and required sporting equipment. The attendant was very kind and knew Langerbrugge College well, as one of the older staff had gone there to help design a new uniform only recently. Green was the predominant colour and soon, the table in front of Ada and Pat was piled high with green skirts and dresses, blouses of the deepest cream, and sweaters with the Langerbrugge crest stitched on. For winter, she presented a bottle-green double-breasted woollen coat and a green beret with kid gloves. The summer blazer was huge, but Aunt Ada insisted that Pat would grow into it. A straw boater finished the summer attire, and they all laughed when Pat placed it jauntily on her head and said, "Ooh la la!"

The lingerie department was next, where Pat was supplied with more underwear than they had altogether at home in Killeshin. She didn't like the look of the green stockings and was proven correct for many years to come, as they itched mercilessly. They continued down to the shoe department, where she tried on black indoor shoes, brown outdoor boots, lacrosse shoes, tennis shoes, and snow boots. Ribbons, hairbands for tennis, and a toiletry valise covered in black leather joined the purchases. Aunt Ada duly filled the toiletry valise with a beautiful silver-backed brush, comb, and mirror set. She and Pat went to the accounts office to pay for their purchases. They arranged for them to be shipped to Belgium as soon as possible, and then it was time to relax.

Ada took her niece by the hand and led her through an ornate wrought-iron room styled like a birdcage and painted a most beautiful shade of azure blue. The birdcage theme carried through the next room, a tearoom with beautifully plumed stuffed birds intertwined amongst the metal bars and creepers. Pat was enchanted and could not believe it when she noticed, in the middle of the tearoom's floor, a smaller version of the birdcage holding two snow-white doves cooing away. The two of them ate freshly made pancakes accompanied by jugs of honey, cream, jam, lemon juice, and whipped chocolate with cups of steaming tea, and soon they felt revived enough to continue shopping for everyday items of clothing.

Aided by two shop porters carrying their numerous parcels, they were soon sitting back, exhausted, in their cab. The assistant from the children's department, with the help of two more porters, carried out additional parcels and new luggage to where another cabby was waiting. Timidly, Pat peered at all the purchases. She was in awe of her new belongings and a little scared that maybe it was really all a dream. Disrupting her daze, Ada let out a great roar of laughter and hugged Pat, thanking her for putting up with all the changing and walking they had done that day. The surreal images of that day would remain engrained in Pat's memory for the rest of her life.

On the journey home to the Tower of London, Pat and Ada stopped again for tea at the Connaught. Totally exhausted, Ada had a glass of deep red wine. She was in such a trance, rabbiting on about their day, that only when the waiter arrived with the food did she notice that Pat was fast asleep, sitting straight up in her chair. She gently woke the girl, and Pat made a brave effort to eat as much as possible, requesting politely that they leave immediately after tea. Soon she was safely in her little bed, dreaming she was back in her Killeshin home, trying to no avail to stuff all her new clothes into the tiny chest of drawers in the bedroom she'd shared with Christine. Waking early the next morning, she gently rubbed her stiff neck and straightened her shoulders to ease the unidentifiable pressure in her chest.

Chapter 9

Leaving London

Pat had developed a stomach pain that seemed to get worse as the days went by. Aunt Ada had arranged for her dear friend Mrs. Goodrum to accompany Pat to the boat to France, as she and Uncle John had to return to Colchester army camp. John had joined them for their last night in London. Hugging her aunt and uncle for the last time upset Pat more than she had thought possible; she felt they were her last connection to home. Through years of training, she had learned to put other people's feelings first, so she tried hard to mask her sadness. Now she had only Mrs. Goodrum to help make her feel secure. Mrs. Goodrum was a very jovial lady who had children of her own. She spent most of their journey to Southampton stitching name tags on the items that had not been sent ahead from London. When she saw Pat anxiously gnawing her nails, she knew it was a sure sign that the girl was finding the change in her life tough going. She was trying her best to display her gratitude toward her aunt and uncle, but it was a struggle—she was only an eleven-year-old girl after all.

Her parents had told her how good Ada and John were to finance her education, and Pat knew this to be true. But in the dark night, while Mrs. Goodrum snored gently beside her, Pat was assailed by torturous thoughts, like tiny demons that jumped and somersaulted around in her brain. Eventually, she fell asleep, exhausted, hot, and blotchy, and the next morning she awoke feeling as though she had never slept. Despite the pangs of loneliness and missing her loving family left behind in Ireland, though, Pat was still brave and spirited for the adventure ahead.

While travelling to Southampton, Pat and Mrs. Goodrum not only practiced French but also had some fun. Aunt Ada had asked her friend to encourage Pat to keep a diary. Pat jotted down notes on all she saw, drawing little pictures in the margins of the pages. The two of them played 'I spy with my little eye', nodding off for little naps between games.

Pat spent a couple of hours reading language cards and practicing French conversation with her companion, who had lived in France for many years. Pat's quick mind really enjoyed the challenge of learning a new language, and soon she began to imagine that she might be able to understand some of what people would say to her in school. Aunt Ada had written to the principal in advance and had received a detailed response, explaining that many young girls travelled to their school without knowing French, and that once immersed in school life, it took very little time for the pupils to become fluent. Pat hadn't believed Aunt Ada when she shared this information, but she had accepted it, more because she needed to than wanted to.

Another train, another goodbye, thought Pat. Mrs. Goodrum had arranged for one of her friends, Eloise Miller, whose husband served with Uncle John, to accompany Pat to Ghent once the boat arrived in France. The British army personnel were well connected, and the families helped each other as much as possible. Pat and Mrs. Goodrum hugged each other, and soon Pat was nearing the final stage of her journey to Langerbrugge.

When she had left England, she felt her life was changing, but she knew this time, the change would be even more dramatic. Her journey across the English Channel was uneventful, yet Pat was troubled by a deep feeling that she couldn't quite identify. Upon reaching Le Havre, Pat heard undistinguishable mumbling, bubbling, and roaring. Soon, it became clear to her that she was entering a new life, at present unknown to her, and in doing so, she would sacrifice all that was near and dear to her, her old life in Killeshin. Straining her ears, she listened to what sounded like an alien language—some people appeared to speak aggressively, while others talked in a soothing purr. However, the dramatic gestures did not always match her interpretations. She kept thinking about her poor little sister Vera, who used to tilt her head in absorbed bafflement. She wondered how Vera was doing and whether Christine was looking after her properly. She missed the little hands that used to hold hers at home. At that moment, Pat would have returned home without a second thought if given the opportunity. Then she spotted a jovial woman, waving open arms and beckoning her. Pat introduced herself to Mrs. Miller, and the two loaded themselves and Pat's belongings into a cab to catch the train.

During the train journey to Ghent, Eloise chatted so incessantly about her children back in England who were attending boarding school that Pat had no regrets about saying goodbye and heading alone to Langerbrugge with the arranged transport. She allowed herself to give vent to her loneliness only as she sat in her bunk at night hugging her beloved cloth bunny. Silent tears rolled down her face until sleep came. Her nail-biting was the only public exhibition of real feeling Pat could allow herself. Her fingers were becoming red, cracked, and raw, but she could not control it.

After Aunt Ada had said goodbye to her niece, she had often doubted the decision to remove such a young girl from all she had ever known and loved. But then she remembered the conversations during the many evenings in the pub when Michael and Ellen had discussed Pat's future. They assured Ada and John that they would know if and when the time was right to decide on Pat's future.

Pat's schoolmaster had written a wonderful letter of introduction to Sister Martha, their contact in Langerbrugge, and Ada re-read it every now and then to reassure herself that she was doing the best she could for her niece. Finally, Pat arrived in Ghent and travelled to the school by arranged transport.

Chapter 10

Meeting Madame Basquille

Langerbrugge School had a huge, handsome granite building, three stories high with numerous sash windows peeking out from behind a magnificent plum, gold, and rust Virginia creeper. A sweeping curve of granite steps bathed in strong autumn sunshine led to green double wooden doors held open by brass lion doorstops. Pat was struck by how the heads of these lions had been rubbed smooth, probably by the many students who had come through the doors over the years. Hesitantly, she lifted her right hand and gently rubbed one of the lion's heads. This action gave her great comfort, as though it would help her fit in. She accompanied Sister Annette, who introduced herself as Madam Basquille's secretary, down the dark, red-tiled hall to the headmistress' office.

Madame Basquille was a petite blonde woman in her fifties. Her hair was softly pulled back in a chignon, and she wore a well-tailored black suit. The only soft relief from the black clothing was a crisp white linen blouse tied in a bow at her neck. Welcoming the new student, she served Sister Annette and Pat tea. Pat watched as Madame Basquille picked up her dainty cup and saucer and made polite conversation. Feeling far too nervous to drink her tea or accept the slice of fruitcake that was on offer, Pat stayed quiet and exercised her manners as best as she could. Every now and again, she caught Sister Annette slipping her a gently reassuring smile. Madame Basquille asked many questions, most seemingly directed at the top of Pat's head. After a while, Pat relaxed a little.

She allowed her gaze to wander, taking in rows of beautiful leather-bound books on large bookshelves, a sizable globe on a brass stand by the bay window, and various coloured velvet wingback chairs on an Aubusson rug. The room had an air of genteel learning, which Pat loved. As she relaxed, she felt her jaw loosen and realised she had been clamping her teeth to stop her lips from betraying any sign of a tremble.

"So, Mademoiselle Fitzpatrick," Madame Basquille spoke directly to Pat, "your luggage has been delivered to the dormitory, and the matron is waiting to settle you in. In a few moments, Sister Annette can take you up."

As Madame Basquille and Sister Annette chatted away, Pat summoned every piece of positive advice she had ever been given, as well as Aunt Ada's parting words, "Think about your little brothers and sisters and loving parents. Each one has made a sacrifice. They did not want you to waste that great mind of yours. They knew it would be difficult for you and difficult for them to let you go. Make them proud of you, and when the time comes, you can help them all." At that moment, Aunt Ada had handed Pat a small parcel wrapped in purple tissue paper, adding, "A little present for you, dear Pat, to help you get to know all your new friends." Inside the parcel was a leather-bound autograph book with a swallow embossed in silver on the top left-hand corner. Recognising the truth of her aunt's advice, Pat resigned herself to making the best of her time in Langerbrugge. Hearing a polite cough from Sister Annette and Madame Basquille, she stood up and followed Sister Annette into the front hall. Just as they were about to go up the staircase, Pat said politely, "Excuse me!" and dashed out the front door, rubbing the brass lion's head again for luck.

Squaring her shoulders, she came back in and climbed the wide, oak staircase with its well-worn red, green, and tan patterned carpet just as the opaque, flame-shaped wall lights in brass holders gently flickered into life. All around her, through the various dormitory doorways, came the mumbling of students. Each dormitory had an ornate name plaque on the front of the door: *Lierre, Houx, Chene, Merle, Coquelicot,* and *Hirondelle.*

She walked up the corridor and finally arrived at her own dormitory. Hirondelle, or swallow, just like the one on her autograph book—*a good omen,* thought Pat. The matron was a tall, sturdy woman with a round face and a ruddy complexion, dressed in a white nurse's uniform. She stood in the dormitory with a large black book, seemingly ticking items off a checklist as she reached each girl's bed, checking they had the correct amount of underwear and nightclothes as per school regulations. At the matron's nod, Pat walked towards what she assumed was her bed, at the end of which were neat piles of underwear and pyjamas. She felt overwhelmed by all the unknown girls' faces, taking in everything about her. That was when the matron took over.

"Now, Mademoiselles, we must welcome our latest arrival, Mademoiselle Pat Fitzpatrick from Ireland."

With that, the girls—most of whom had been at the school from an early age—burst into applause and smiled at Pat. Suddenly, the dormitory transformed from an unknown territory into a place filled with warmth and possibilities. All too soon, the glow of welcome dissipated when the applause ceased, and the girls turned back to their various tasks.

At first, not knowing French was a huge barrier. Pat went up to the white locker beside her bed and placed her autograph book on the little shelf, determined to learn the language as quickly as possible, no matter what. Looking around the long dormitory room, she took in the two rows of ten beds facing each other. There was a long sash window between each bed with a white locker underneath. The curtains were made of thick red fabric, adorned with multiple flowers. As the matron drew the heavy curtains, the lights in the room emphasised the soft sheen of a herringbone parquet floor. Time began to trickle by.

Soon, the days had turned into weeks, and Pat focused on her books, trying with the greatest effort to absorb the French language. At every free moment, she withdrew to the farthest corner of the school library, mumbling away to herself in French. As she retreated more and more into her own little world, she sometimes overheard some of her new classmates speaking about her in hushed tones. As she didn't know the language, she assumed they were talking about her in an unkind way. Pat had a constant knot in the pit of her stomach, a knot that kept swelling and surging as she contemplated the fact that she was alone.

After a while, her imagination conjured up a make-believe friend with whom she would chat about her family and home. The nuns noticed that Pat was beginning to get a reputation for being a bit odd. She seemed lost.

Chapter 11

The Autograph Book

It was the first of November. Pat could not believe that she had been in her Belgium boarding school for such a long time. Maybe it was the sweet scent of burning leaves and the nearly hypnotic effect of the yellowish-grey, pink-tinged light that appears only at that time of year. She stopped on her way back to her dormitory, having collected a forgotten book. Standing with her back to her small cast-iron bed, Pat allowed her thoughts to drift back to her beloved home. The muscles in her stomach tightened as she let out a long, deep sigh at the memory of her last day at home, lying alongside her mother in the old Killeshin hill graveyard, holding her hand, feeling her skin, catching a gentle whiff of her perfume. She recalled the tinkling of her little brothers' and sisters' laughter as they chased each other about the fields. How safe she had felt then, surrounded by all things familiar. Her reverie was interrupted by a sudden swoosh of fabric. Pat turned swiftly on her heel to see the stern face of Sister Dominique.

"Now, now, Mademoiselle Fitzpatrick." The nun's nostrils widened as she raised her chin as if to identify some foul smell. "You are not here to be self-indulgent or sad. Major Colgan has not sacrificed all his money for this."

Clapping her hands, Sister Dominique moved aside to let Pat pass and then followed her all the way to the study area. As the girl slid as discreetly as possible into her study seat, she caught sight of Sister Dominique whispering to Mademoiselle Vert, the study mistress. The students eyed Pat with curiosity, making her feel isolated. For the next few hours, she was afraid to look up in case she attracted Mademoiselle's attention.

The study hall was very warm on that mild afternoon. Time passed slowly, and light turned to darkness; the ticking of the clock over Mademoiselle's desk served as a constant reminder to Pat that she was here to study and not daydream about home. Putting pen to paper, she totally lost herself in French verbs and comprehension, intermittently pausing to chew her thumbnails.

Finally, the bell rang for tea. Pat quickly scooped up her books, tucked them under her arm, and tried to become submerged in the swell of the queue surging towards the door. "Mademoiselle Fitzpatrick!" the study mistress called.

Pat stood and waited for further reprimands. The study mistress watched as each pupil left the room until it was completely empty, making Pat even more apprehensive.

Finally, the study mistress spoke: "Here at Langerbrugge, it is the tradition to achieve the highest academic results from our pupils as is possible. You, Mademoiselle Fitzpatrick, have fitted so well into this world. You have worked at every single element of your studies with Trojan effort. Now you need to learn to relax just a little. It cannot be easy for you coming from Ireland without knowing the language or anything about this school. When I was young, I was also sent to boarding school. My advice is to take time to bond with all the wonderful girls here. The great friends I met in boarding school made me feel like I had a second family. This is where you will begin to build such meaningful relationships, those that will last a lifetime."

Having expected to be scolded, Pat was surprised when Mademoiselle gave her a quick hug and told her to hurry on or there would be no tea left. This was the advice that Pat really needed. Being a conscientious girl, she had put all her efforts into her books and study, yet she knew she needed more contact with the other girls. She knew it was the only thing that might ease her deep homesickness. She raced upstairs to change her shoes, and as she slipped off the bed to fetch her indoor pumps from underneath, she spotted the leather-bound autograph book on her locker shelf. Aunt Ada's words came back to her about using the book to make new friends. The girl in the bed beside Pat's seemed approachable; she had been grinning at her on and off since Pat had arrived at Langerbrugge. A petite girl with long black plaits, she now sat across from Pat, swinging her stockinged feet, smiling and humming a gentle tune.

Right, thought Pat. *She looks kind.*

Picking up her autograph book, she approached the girl timidly. "Hello, my name is Pat. I wondered if you could be the first to put your name in my book." That began one of Pat's lifelong friendships. The girl's name was Nicole Lievre, and she was from outside Paris. When she wrote in Pat's autograph book, she drew a cartoon image of herself with a bubble coming out of her mouth saying, "Friends forever true." Pat then asked her to write her birthday. She could not believe it when she saw 18 June 1897—Pat's own birth date. She felt it was a good omen. Pat emitted a small squeal of delight, the first of many such squeals she would make during the remainder of her time in Langerbrugge.

Soon, there was a small queue waiting to autograph Pat's book. She felt the tension in her stomach ease. Things weren't so bad after all. The matron finally intervened and said they must all go down to tea. Nicole took Pat by the arm and pulled her towards the dormitory door, all the while chatting in a mixture of English and French, which Pat found amusing and confusing at the same time.

Walking down the long corridors in the basement of the old house was always eerie, as there were no windows. The lighting was made up of baton-like strips in the middle of the low ceiling. The green-coloured emulsion paint and rubberised flooring were grim.

But when Nicole opened the door into the dining hall, it looked like Christmas dinner was being served. There were large glass dome lights hanging over numerous trestle tables with benches and queue upon queue of students ranging from around seven years of age to eighteen. The noise was deafening; everyone spoke as if they would never get the chance to speak again. Five serving ladies stood behind large, steaming vats, ladling out food to each student. As it was teatime, eggs seemed to be the most popular—scrambled, boiled, or poached with mountains of toast, a large glass of milk, and two little biscuits.

Nicole instructed Pat to take a piece of fruit from the large bowls on the side tables and then led her towards a table by the grandfather clock. Every girl placed her heaping tray in front of her and remained standing in complete silence until Madame Basquille started prayers.

The entire experience was fascinating to Pat. Her heart had opened to new opportunities, and that was when her thirst for adventure really began to take hold.

The autograph book with its embossed silver swallow on the leather cover was to remain with Pat for the rest of her life. Each page held the name of a girl who became a precious friend. Time passed quickly. Everything Pat did was fresh and exciting, and she really wanted to immerse herself in her new world.

However, school life was full of challenges. She had never before encountered many of the subjects she was expected to master. Pat had expected that learning a new language would be difficult, but she was really challenged by having to use the dictionary constantly, as some words had multiple meanings. She often felt frustrated, but her new friends kept her going. Games of lacrosse and tennis and school drama productions were great outlets, where she could relax and enjoy herself. Pat was not the school's only English-speaking student, but Madame Basquille had obviously instructed the school staff and older girls to make sure that English speakers had little opportunity to chat in their native tongue. Nevertheless, the girls developed a code of facial expressions to let each other know that they objected to not being allowed to spend time together. Whenever these exchanges were discovered by Sister Dominique, she would deliver one of her notorious heart-freezing glares, which would frighten the culprits and force them to behave, at least for a while.

The grounds around Langerbrugge provided Pat solace. Out there, she could just run and skip to the sound of the wind or bird song. She revelled in the many earthy smells of the little hedges and flower beds. The sweet summer scent of lavender became her favourite. The nuns showed the girls how to make little linen pouches tied with ribbon, which they could fill with dried lavender. Placing these in their chest of drawers provided not just a relaxing fragrance but protected their clothes from moths.

Langerbrugge was full of beautiful trees and little paths leading to various statues of the Virgin Mary and Christ. Gardeners planted seasonal flower beds—grape hyacinths, crocuses, daffodils, and narcissus in the spring; blue and white lobelia with red begonias in the summer; chrysanthemums of rust and yellow for autumn, and red and white cyclamens in the winter. Pat loved being outside, no matter how inclement the weather. The nuns encouraged the girls to stop and pray on walks and outings. Pat relished this time where she could just be quiet and alone. Sometimes, while looking up into the eyes of the religious statues, she imagined she was back with her family in the old church on Killeshin Hill. As a small child, she had developed a habit of staring into the faces of the various saints. If she stared long enough, she had been told by whispering friends, she just might see the statue's eyes move or observe tears falling from them. Nothing like this ever happened, which came as a relief, as Pat wasn't sure how she would deal with it if it did.

Every Saturday, the nuns allowed each of the students one sheet of writing paper and a stamped envelope. Pat always managed to write more than anyone else, as she developed a tiny writing style, not only straight down the page, but also all around the edges. Her letters were packed with enthusiasm and cheerfulness. Aunt Ada's parting words as they said their last goodbye always reverberated in her mind, ensuring that Pat kept all her angst to herself. It was only when she had finished her letter and handed it up to the study mistress for posting that Pat allowed that homesick feeling to surface. Then she would chew her nails and make her way to the nearest bathroom to cry, out of sight of prying eyes.

Monday mornings always started with PE. It was a great start to each week and helped Pat get over the quietness and solitude of the very religious Sunday routine, which usually left her feeling homesick. To her, Sunday represented family. Her loneliness was exacerbated when some local girls, who attended as weekday boarders, went home on a Friday to return full of happy stories on Sunday evening. As far as Pat was concerned, on Monday mornings, the harsh sound of the PE mistress, Mademoiselle Durr, shouting and blowing her whistle to announce team names, provided something of a comfort—it meant she could just get on with things and forget sad thoughts. For the rest of the week, routine followed routine, broken only by the occasional visit of sports teams from nearby schools. Thursday evening choir practice, led by Sister Dominique, was a sign that the week was finally coming to an end.

On Friday afternoons, which started at 12:30 p.m., the girls would have a quick lunch of soup and rolls, and afterwards rush up to their dorms to change into their Sunday clothes and outdoor shoes or boots. The matron inspected each girl to check that her uniform was perfect. Nobody could leave the school until she was satisfied.

She looked Pat up and down, slowly taking in the straight hair parted in the middle with its fringe just dusting below her eyebrows. After inspecting the bottle-green, double-breasted woollen belted coat, green beret and kid gloves, brown stockings, and well-polished outdoor shoes, the matron let her leave with the rest of the girls.

Feeling relieved, Pat ran down the driveway and out the black gates with the five girls she had come to regard as her dearest friends. They linked arms and hummed their favourite songs together. It was only after

Halloween that these girls were allowed to spend time together, as they were the ones who originated from native English-speaking countries. In pale winter sunlight with the winter's crisp leaves crunching underfoot, the girls planned what they would buy to eat in the little village shops. They breathed in the freezing November air, blowing out plumes of smoke, laughing and joking as they pretended to be smoking cigarettes. These were very happy times, but even so, Pat sometimes felt a little guilty.

The village of Langerbrugge was compact. At the end of it, the butcher, the baker, and the sweet shop were nestled next to a little granite stone church and graveyard. Small two-storey houses ran along either side of a street that led to a horse trough and water pump, conveniently located next to the blacksmith's shop and the local school. In the middle of the village stood a granite cross, commemorating those who lost their lives at war. Every Friday afternoon, a market took place, adding to the atmosphere and novelty of the weekly outing. All types of trinkets were on offer for a pittance, including ribbons, knitted hats, scarves and gloves, sweets, and beautifully embroidered linen.

By Christmas, life had settled into a busy routine that Pat—or Winnie as some of the girls called her—found she really thrived on. Mademoiselle Vert congratulated her as she handed her a bundle of her exam results. "You have worked well Mademoiselle Fitzpatrick; your family will be delighted. Major Colgan and his wife have been sent a copy of your results also. We are all very happy to see that you have made many friends. Each teacher has nothing but praise for you. Well done."

This praise was just what Pat needed. She felt she had wonderful friends in Langerbrugge, but she had to deal with not only criticism but racism as well. Many a time, as is typical with cowards, the principle, Madame Basquille, hid her contempt of Pat under a cloak of sarcasm. "Qui, Mademoiselle Fitzpatrick, how could a petite Irish colleen understand the complicated workings of the French language? The accent, what can I say?" she would purr as she pouted her red lipstick-painted mouth and raised her pert nose even higher, patting down her blonde chignon as if this action itself would erase Pat's pathetic attempts to master French. During verbal tests, she entered the classroom to stand, arms folded, until Pat stuttered her way through each verb, afterwards giving the teacher a sympathetic glance as she tip-tapped swiftly out of the room.

Sister Dominique always seemed to be around during Pat's worst moments, when she felt as though she was never going to master the language. She encouraged her to chat as often as possible with the French-born girls. She told her that the only way was to listen—eventually, her ear would pick up the many sounds that made perfect French. She also took to leaving notes on Pat's locker with any corrections she had noticed were needed. As was the way with many nuns, an almost maternal relationship built up over the years between Pat and Sister Dominique. The kindness this teacher showed the girls provided a very secure atmosphere, helping Pat gain enough confidence and knowledge to win the annual gold medal for French in school the following year. The almost saintly look of satisfaction on Sister Dominique's face as Madame Basquille presented Pat with her medal cemented Pat's determination to do well at everything. The day Pat received her medal, not only had she Sister Dominique's support but also that of her "Autograph Girls", as they called themselves, who clapped and cheered her. The *Hirondelle* autograph book created a lasting bond between Pat and her five friends. The symbol of the swallow on this little leather keepsake represented freedom to all of them. She had tasted a new life where she had responsibility only to herself. It was up to her to make the best of her opportunities. Pat had come to realise that this new world was where she wanted to be. The new world meant everything to her, but most of all it represented freedom.

In Ireland, she had been entrusted with responsibility for her younger siblings. This was the way it had always been with her, Mother being so ill most of the time. It had been quite a shock to have all control taken from her when she arrived at Langerbrugge. She had felt frightened. Now she knew that if she worked hard, she would be able to achieve even more independence. The girls knew most of her family history and were sympathetic, but it was Mabel Graham's piece in the autograph book that resonated most with Pat.

Mabel's family were English and worked for the foreign office. They had sent Mabel to Langerbrugge in 1910, a year before Pat arrived. Both girls loved the outdoor life and spent a lot of their time writing about nature. This was how Mabel came to write in Pat's autograph book in November 1911.

"The inner side of every cloud
Is bright and shining,
Therefore, turn your clouds about
And always wear them inside out
To show the lining."

Chapter 12

Foreign Christmas

Christmas 1911 was the first of many that Pat would spend away from Ireland. It had been arranged that she, along with many other foreign students, would spend the holidays in Langerbrugge. Once the winter exams were over, preparation began for what was, for many, the most important event in the school calendar, the Christmas play. Each form had to prepare and present a ten-minute play with a Christmas theme. Pat had been planning a production with her "Autograph Girls". It kept her busy. Her only major distraction was a parcel from Killeshin that contained individually wrapped little gifts from each family member as well as a long, news-filled letter from Mother. Reading the letter made her feel a knot of homesickness in her stomach. Biting her thumbnail, she read every line, which created a vivid image of each individual. They had been planning this parcel since the end of September. For once, they had been allowed in the good room, where Father had placed a large piece of oilcloth on the parquet floor to protect it from any paint or glue. Christine had knitted a red woollen hat with a black bobbin on top along with matching mittens. Inside a mitten, Pat found a little note telling her how much she missed her. The same note informed her that Vera was to go into a home as the family could no longer help her. Pat felt sad but also a sense of relief; deep down, she had always known it would have to happen eventually. Tears rolled down her face as she pictured little Vera's sweet expression.

Among the other gifts, Pat unwrapped a one-penny bar from Paddy, a pressed flower picture from Gertie, a wooden pencil-case from John, which he had made with help, an orange from Scholastica, and handprint of Kitty's in blue ink on velum. Each present came with a homemade card. Finally, Pat unwrapped a large tin of Fry's pure cocoa, a gift from her parents. The accompanying card read, "We know you miss us as much we miss you, but nothing could please us more than giving our scholar such a wonderful opportunity. You are as loved as always. Mother."

Pat had already discovered during her first term at Langerbrugge that keeping busy was the best cure for sorrow. She put all her energy into the forthcoming play.

The "Autograph Girls" wrote and produced a small play called *Christmas for Girls 1911*. The play was based on *The Illustrated London News*, Christmas, 1911. The magazine was a very popular publication from England that Mabel's parents had sent over to the school. The girls made a replica of the magazine's famous picture-frame logo large enough to hold the entire group of twelve. The girls who did not wish to be on stage had plenty of jobs to do. Irene was the cherub-like girl in the cover picture. She sat on a velvet chair with the rest of the girls around her wearing pretty dresses from the props room. In the magazine, the girls had noted a new fashion trend—women were wearing trousers. Inspired by this, Pat arrived on stage to end the production in wide black trousers and a white shirt, with tinsel in her hair, carrying a placard calling for "Votes for Women."

This caused quite a stir in the school assembly hall, and the nuns were shocked. Later Madame Basquille told the girls they had gone too far. However, Mademoiselle Fitzpatrick, who had masterminded the production, was on fire with resolve to be part of this strong new movement.

Chapter 13

First World War, Langerbrugge, 1914

The Reverend Mother placed the telegram on her desk. Then she rolled her rosary beads between her fingers, allowing herself a few moments of peaceful reflection before raising them to her lips to kiss the dangling cross. Opening the top drawer, she removed a small blue vial of angina medication, and took not one but two of the tablets, washing them down with the last drops of her cold tea. For many months, since Reverend Mother had taken over from Madame Basquille, there had been whispers of the probability of war between Kaiser Wilhelm's Germany and Europe. Certain foodstuffs were in short supply. German soldiers had marched into Belgium and were now close by and positioned in and around Ghent. The telegram from one of their sister convents in neutral Switzerland brought news of terrible atrocities the Germans were committing elsewhere. It also contained an offer of accommodation for the college's teachers and pupils. Her decision made, Reverend Mother placed the medication vial in her habit pocket. They would leave the following morning.

On 30 August 1914, the staff and students gathered in the dining room. Each girl stood at her year table, head bowed in prayer. Earlier, Reverend Mother had met with all the sisters and very firmly explained what was happening and what they each needed to do. Taking out a small notebook and pencil from the pocket of her habit, Sister Canus took notes, licking her pencil every now and then, a sign that she was worried. Reverend Mother was very glad that these women had been working alongside her at the college. She knew she could trust them to put their own fears last. Just before they dispersed to gather the girls and inform the kitchen and various other staff members of their plans, she raised her hand to address them. "I am sure there is no need to remind you, but we need to appear as calm and confident as possible. One sniff of fear from any of us, and we will have a group of hysterical females on our hands, which could really slow us down. We don't know if the authorities will try to stop us, and we all need to appear unworried. We will be telling the border guards that this is a school trip that we organised earlier in the year. Remember to inform the girls that it is their parents' and guardians' decision. Be firm. I want you to choose three students from the senior years and give them the full information. We will need their support. Can we decide now on which three girls are most suited?"

Without hesitation, the nuns put names forward. "Mademoiselle Fitzpatrick, Mademoiselle Ruisse, and Mademoiselle Neff," came the reply from each sister in turn. There was no more time to discuss the matter. They spontaneously blessed themselves and left to attend to their tasks.

Sister Canus sent petite Isabelle to ask the three girls to come to the dining hall. The three students got on extremely well with Sister Canus, who never felt the need to conform to rules unless she believed it absolutely necessary. Pat and the other two spent many an evening with her, hidden in the shed behind the kitchen where she had introduced them to the secrets of the tarot cards as well as the occasional cigarette. Indeed, the tarot cards remained an influence throughout Pat's life, and upon several occasions, they even proved to be a lifesaver.

The students quickly took in all that Sister Canus said, the shock showing in their young faces. "Girls, I know you are really taken aback by this quick decision, but believe me, there is no other option. We cannot risk staying any longer, and you need to be so brave."

Gathering the three girls in her bony arms, she hugged them and told them to stand and wait for the mealtime gong.

The dining hall was full when Reverend Mother rang her silver bell. Once the students realised that there would be no food until after her speech, silence descended quickly. The Reverend Mother did not give many details except that they were to pack quickly and bring just essential clothing and personal mementoes. She directed a couple of sisters to attend to girls she could see were becoming teary. "Remember girls, your parents and guardians have requested this trip, so we cannot disappoint them."

Then she instructed them all to sit down. Immediately, plates of bread and butter went around, along with some cheese from the local dairy. All the girls received a glass of milk and the advice to eat and drink as much as they could, as they were to leave at sunrise without breakfast.

Sister Camilla was the school's music teacher. She stood and took her place on the raised podium beside Reverend Mother and the rest of the nuns. Reverend Mother finished her speech by wishing them all a safe journey and sat down, whereupon Sister Camilla started to sing in her clear, strong voice. She had chosen "Keep the Home Fires Burning", a song written by Ivor Novello that she had heard some students singing when she was in Britain for holidays earlier that summer. The words of this song were comforting yet thought-provoking. Many of the girls and the nuns had family who were actively taking part in this war, and it was not long before many of them hummed along, several with tears rolling down their faces.

Pat knew of a number of families in Co Laois whose sons, fathers, uncles, or other relatives had recently joined the British army. Her mother always included such local details in her letters. Aunt Ada had written to tell Pat that Uncle John was on active service. Being able to put a human face to the war made Pat very proud but also very aware of the dangers. One such family were the Nelsons from down the road. Pat remembered them as being older with a great affinity with animals, especially horses. Her mother said young Jack Nelson had become a member of King Edward's Horse regiment, which was no surprise knowing his skill.

Once the singing was over, the girls silently went up the stairs to sleep with their clothes on, boots placed alongside their beds to be put on quickly early the following morning.

Nobody really slept that night, and certainly Pat did not. She was up before the nuns rang the morning bell, fully prepared and helping the younger girls who were whinging with tiredness and fear. She carried the smallest girl down to the hall and handed her case to a driver from one of the buses waiting outside the main door. Then she climbed on to sit beside the driver. Once the buses were full, the drivers closed the doors, and the buses pulled away.

Digging her nails into her closed palms, her stomach churning in fear, Pat turned slowly for a last look back at her beloved school, a place she had become very happy to regard as home.

Chapter 14

Switzerland 1914

The buses carrying the school group arrived at the train station, where the stationmaster greeted them. He knew Reverend Mother well from her frequent journeys to Switzerland to visit the order's other convent. It was mayhem. By now the younger girls were fully awake; each seemed to be trying to outdo the other by crying loudest. Hunger pangs had also set in. Nothing the sisters said or threatened made any difference. People kept glancing their way in disgust and tut-tutting, letting the stationmaster know just how annoying they found the unseemly racket of over a hundred girls of various ages, most of them weeping and surrounded by their baggage. On an ordinary day, the sight of nuns scurrying about desperately trying to placate the girls could have been quite amusing, but this was no ordinary day—the winds of war were blowing, creating anxiety everywhere. However, the chaos eventually worked to the nuns' advantage, as the stationmaster used the chaos as an excuse to hurry the students, nuns, and staff onto the train quickly. He allowed Reverend Mother to show all the gathered passports while he just took a quick head count. She slipped him a discreet tip as she made a great fuss of taking both his hands in hers, thanking him profusely and promising to pray for himself and his family forevermore. They exchanged solemn looks, fully aware they probably would never meet again.

Although it was still bright when they boarded the train, the nuns unwrapped the parcels of homemade bread, breaking it into small pieces. Next, they opened flasks of warm milk and poured some into the metal mugs they had brought with them, adding bread and a pinch of precious sugar, mashing it together before carefully handing it to the youngest students first. The tears had dried the minute the girls got on the train, when they saw the nuns and staff preparing their food. The older girls waited impatiently, afraid the food supplies would run out. They knew that Goody never lasted long, especially as the pinch of sugar made it extra tasty. Reverend Mother knew from experience that Goody was perfect for supper, as it not only filled the students' stomachs but made them sleepy. Once everyone had eaten, she called for night prayers. The girls were exhausted and spoke not one word as they prepared for bed. They were so glad to climb into their bunks to sleep.

Swishing the curtains closed around her as she climbed up to the top bunk of the railway carriage, Pat finally allowed herself to feel how exhausted she was. She was never tired enough, though, to miss out on the chance of quiet moments while everyone was asleep. She sat cross-legged on her bunk, and taking her small satchel from under her pillow, she removed her little silver battery torch. She had packed most of her belongings into the trunk Aunt Ada had purchased for her in London, but she made sure to keep her personal papers in her brown leather satchel, which held her passport, her last letter from home, her diary, and the small autograph book, which contained some dried flowers from the college garden and messages from friends as well as various items she had cut out from magazines and newspapers. Her favourite was a war poem written by Jesse Pope called "War Girls", which she found inspirational:

"There's the motor girl who drives a heavy van.

There's the butcher girl who brings your joint of meat."

It was so different from the La Belle Époque years that reflected life in Europe before the war, when young ladies learned to run a home and tend to their men and children competently once they made a decent marriage. Reading this poem over and over, she was aware that life was changing for women. To Pat, the idea that earning her own money could give her independence made her determined to make a life for herself and not settle for one in which she was reliant on a husband.

She placed the items from her satchel on her bed and slid her hand behind the brown silk lining of the bag to take out the tarot cards that Sister Canus had given to her for safekeeping. She did not want any of the other sisters to know about her interest, as the church frowned upon tarot cards. The girls had only just begun to learn about the cards and their meanings when they were forced to leave Belgium. They had been fascinated, and Sister Canus had taken great delight in cloaking the cards in as much mystery and suspense as she could. Slipping under the covers with her satchel beside her pillow, Pat placed the cards and torch under the bedcover to wait until Reverend Mother had checked on all the older students and wished them goodnight. The bed felt scratchy. There was a slightly stale smell from the curtains. Pat stayed very still as she waited for the chance to discover what the cards might tell her. Torch on and with cards placed, she studied each one and tried to convince herself that she knew what she was doing. A long, happy, and exciting life lay ahead of her—or so she decided. Then she gave in and lay down to sleep, pleasantly conscious of the rocking of the carriage.

Chapter 15

Swiss Life

Anyone waiting on the platform for their morning train at the Bahnhofplatz in Bern on 31 August 1914 would have been fascinated by the arrival of the chugging steam train carrying the students from Langerbrugge. Eager to see their new home, the students had been up since early that morning. The night before, Reverend Mother had instructed them to wash their faces and hands with the flannels that Sister Canus had soaked and rinsed out with precious water provided by the train's porter. The younger girls had formed a queue and stood patiently while older students quickly and a little roughly scrubbed their faces and hands. Excitement had overtaken their indignation at this treatment. Now rows of pink, shiny faces beamed out the carriage windows, the girls waving at anyone who even appeared to glance their way. People could not help but respond warmly. Their eager little faces pressed up to the window glass created a very jovial, amusing picture. It was a glorious morning with blue skies and trees lit up with dappled sunshine. A gentle breeze seemed to whistle to Pat in greeting as herself and her two friends assisted the girls off the train and toward the jolly porter who was busily taking the luggage from various compartments. He placed it all beside Reverend Mother and Sister Canus, who was diligently counting bags and suitcases and then re-counting them and checking them against her list.

Aunt Pat's War

Pat had never seen anything like the geraniums that sat prettily in the station's window boxes. They were vivid red, a perfect contrast to the high-gloss black planters. The station floor was so clean that you could have eaten off it. Indeed, everything seemed to gleam.

Finally, they were all disembarked and ready. Taking their luggage from Sister Canus, they made an orderly way through the station gates. Mother Luca from their new home was waiting outside the station with the convent caretaker, Hal, who was very small and skinny. Alongside Hal was the farm manager, Sister Alberta, known as Berta, a large lady with a huge chest and quite an amazing beard. Sister Canus had forewarned Pat and the two girls who oversaw the younger girls to be on high alert to prevent any untoward comments. The only preventative that had any effect was a threat to tell Reverend Mother, which thankfully worked, even if it didn't stop a few suppressed giggles escaping now and again. They filled the trunks of two buses with the many bags.

Once all the students were on the buses and the headcount was taken, they drove off to their new home, which was five miles outside Bern.

Sitting at last on the bus with everyone, too exhausted to speak, Pat reflected on what was making her feel strange. Her gut feeling told her that the atmosphere was different in Switzerland—so happy and calm. As the tension ebbed away from her, she became aware that she was smiling, yes, actually smiling. Up to that point, she hadn't realised that the threat of war had such an adverse effect on her. Around her, the rest of the students appeared equally relaxed. It was a slightly bumpy, uphill journey, but Pat's heart soared as they passed through the most beautiful green pastures. Huge, well-fed, tan-skinned cows with big metal bells hung around their necks looked at them with sweeping, long-lashed eyes as they nonchalantly chewed the rich grass. Pat loved it. The rural landscape reminded her of Killeshin, and although it was very different to Co Laois, it had a similar calming effect. Breathing in the smell of grass, animals, and a sweet hint of alpine flowers, she knew she was going to be happy here.

The buses pulled up outside several two-storeyed chalets clustered together in a little courtyard enclave with a well and a pump in the centre. Reverend Mother announced, "Welcome to your new home, girls."

Without another word, they surged from the buses and started running around, squealing with excitement. The teachers decided to leave them alone for the moment. They knew the girls needed to let off steam after all the tension and confinement of travel throughout the previous day and a half. The nuns went into the head chalet with their Swiss sisters, leaving Pat and the older girls to keep an eye on the younger students. On the outside of the enclave, ten goats stood around in pens, peering at the girls with great curiosity. Next to the goats was a large wooden chicken coop. Chickens of various sizes and colours ran all around the yard while a huge cockerel strutted about, fixing his piercing gaze on the next object of his affection. The girls had already captured two sheepdogs and were busily hugging and petting these docile canines. Meanwhile, troublemaker Dorothy Mires had found a small comb in her pocket and was attempting to put her hair ribbon on one of the dog's silky manes when Pat stopped her. The other girls laughed, and this laughter quickly became infectious and spread. Soon, everyone had joined in.

After the fun and laughter died down, the girls waited to be called in for food, as they were beginning to feel very hungry. A sister rang a large bell by the main door with great enthusiasm, and the girls formed orderly queues and prepared to go inside for tea. What a meal it was! The food was so fresh. Jugs of cold cow's milk, plates of hard-boiled eggs and goats' cheese along with crispy rolls covered in creamy butter. Not a sound could be heard in the room, and neither was there a crumb left on a plate. The younger girls were nearly falling into their dishes with exhaustion when Reverend Mother stood and made the sign of cross, thanking God for their safe arrival and generous hosts.

After a quick wash and a general tidy-up, everyone—even the nuns—headed to bed, such was the relief and effect of their traumatic adventure. As usual, Pat waited until everyone was asleep before taking out her torch and writing in her diary. She wanted to remember every detail about this amazing place to put in the next letter she wrote home. That night, she was so exhausted that she never even felt Sister Canus remove and close her diary and switch off her torch, placing it gently beside the bed. Pulling the covers over Pat's shoulders, she paused for a moment and reflected on the child she should have had if life had not interfered and taken her one chance away.

Chapter 16

In Love

Smoothing down her tweed trousers and pinching her cheeks to make herself look alert and not love-tussled, Pat arrived at Reverend Mother's office door. She knocked hesitantly, and then she waited until she was told to enter.

Inside, Pat stood, holding her breath as Reverend Mother slowly took her glasses off her nose and placed them on her desk. "Ah, Pat, you look well. We don't see as much of you now as we used to. I am very pleased with your Christmas exam results. As usual, your languages are excellent and you have made great progress, especially in maths. As you know, your guardians Colonel and Mrs Colgan have written to me many times about your future. Although they have always provided for you and will continue to do so, they are most insistent that you will leave this college with the means to earn a living. I have given this matter a lot of thought, and the sisters and I have formulated a plan that we feel will fulfil your great potential as well as the wishes of your guardians."

She beckoned Pat to sit in a chair in front of her desk. Pat finally let out her breath slowly as she realised she had not been summoned because of Pieter. She had become friendly with one of the local girls who was a day boarder. Eve had a handsome brother called Pieter, and it was not long before Pat and Pieter started seeing each other. They spent their time walking in the mountains and talking about how they felt about each other. Pat now wore Pieter's scarf at every opportunity. She had never experienced anything like it and thought about nothing but when she would see Pieter again. Having spent the entire weekend at Eve's home, she and Pieter, with Eve's help, had managed to escape to spend time together without a chaperone. If the nuns found out, there would be a lot of trouble. Pat was afraid of anything that would interfere with her precious time with Pieter.

Opening the folder beside her, Reverend Mother told Pat that she had arranged for her to leave the college for a couple of weeks to train as a tutor in Geneva. Pat thought she would burst with emotion. "But Reverend Mother, I cannot do that," she stammered and then blushed profusely, realising that she was being stared at intently. "Thank you so much, Reverend Mother. But the little girls will miss me so much that I feel I just cannot leave them."

She wanted to say more, but for once she fell silent as she tried to construct the most impressive argument possible. Her thoughts were interrupted abruptly when the headmistress slammed the folder shut. The Reverend Mother then spoke in the strongest tone Pat had ever heard her use. "No, Miss Pat. You will go to Geneva on the Friday afternoon train. Sister Basil from the University of Geneva will meet you there. You will stay with her at her rooms, and she will guide you the entire time you will spend there. I am telling you it is in your best interests. It is decided. There is no need for further discussion."

By now, Pat was fully aware that anything she said would make no difference at all. One look at Reverend Mother's set-in-stone face made her realise she knew all about Pieter and the secret weekend meetings. What a shock! Pat thought her heart would burst as she left to start preparing for her departure on Friday. She nearly tripped, trying to escape from the office as quickly as possible.

Once outside the office, she broke into a run, changing her route and going as fast as she could. She could not wait to tell Eve and Liza her terrible news. Nothing the girls said gave Pat any comfort. She was so distraught that her friends persuaded her to plead illness and spend the rest of the day in her room, where she wrote one of the saddest letters a teenager in love could ever write. Handing the note to Eve, Pat waited until she was in her bed that night and all the dormitory lights were out before she cried again. She had never felt so low. Waking at six the following morning, she felt ill—sore head, sore eyes, sore throat. But she had to ignore this, as she knew that Eve would have given Pieter her message when she got home, and he would turn up at their usual meeting place. Quickly putting on her clothes and raking her fingers through her hair, she headed for the back door where she kept her heavy boots. She had woken so early that only Hal, the farm manager, was up. He was tending to the animals, though, and thus easy to avoid.

She trudged through the snow in the hazy pre-dawn light and down the little path to the shepherd's shelter, as it was known. Pieter was waiting for her. They flung their arms around each other as their tears mingled.

"I cannot bear it, Pieter. Geneva is so far away, and who knows what other plans they have for me. What will we do?"

But Eve had told her mother about Pat being sent to Geneva, and she had spent many hours the night before talking to Pieter, trying to get him to understand that they were too young, and Pat would be in a position to earn her own money once trained to be a tutor. She added that he would soon have to leave to become a border guard, as the family's money was short, and border guards received food and lodgings in addition to generous pay. The number of troops from both sides crossing into Switzerland by mistake meant they were constantly recruiting. She had pleaded with him to be strong, emphasising that Reverend Mother would not tolerate any interference with her plan for Pat and that he needed to be unselfish and not make things even harder on her. He had his family to support him, whereas Pat had only the school, and the nuns were never going to approve of their relationship.

"You can meet Pat again when you have both matured a little more. It will all work out. If it is meant to be, it will be," she promised him.

Eve had told Pieter that Reverend Mother could easily send Pat back home to Ireland. In fact, she had taken precisely that action when another girl had fallen for a local boy the previous month. Obviously, Reverend Mother thought highly of Pat's potential, or she would not have gone to so much trouble to not only separate her from Pieter but also to organise for Pat the best possible further education.

Pat could not believe Pieter's attitude as he spoke gently yet firmly to her. His words were all about the future, indicating they should wait until they were older. As he stroked her head, she could feel herself turning first bright red with anger, then white with sorrow.

"You liar. You don't love me at all!" she screamed as she ran blindly from the shepherd's hut with Pieter staring after her in dejection and defeat.

FIGURE 1: Kitty smoking in the flat.

ENGLISH HOME

English lady receives paying guests in large modern villa giving on the sea three miles from Deauville

GOOD BATHING – TENNIS – RIDING, etc.

TERMS MODERATE

Apply : W. FITZ PATRICK

8, Villa Guizot
PARIS 17·

Villa Durenne
VILLERS-sur-MER (Calvados)
Téléphone 703-75

FIGURE 2: Advertisement for Pat's Guesthouse 'Villa Durenne' in Villiers-sur-Mer.

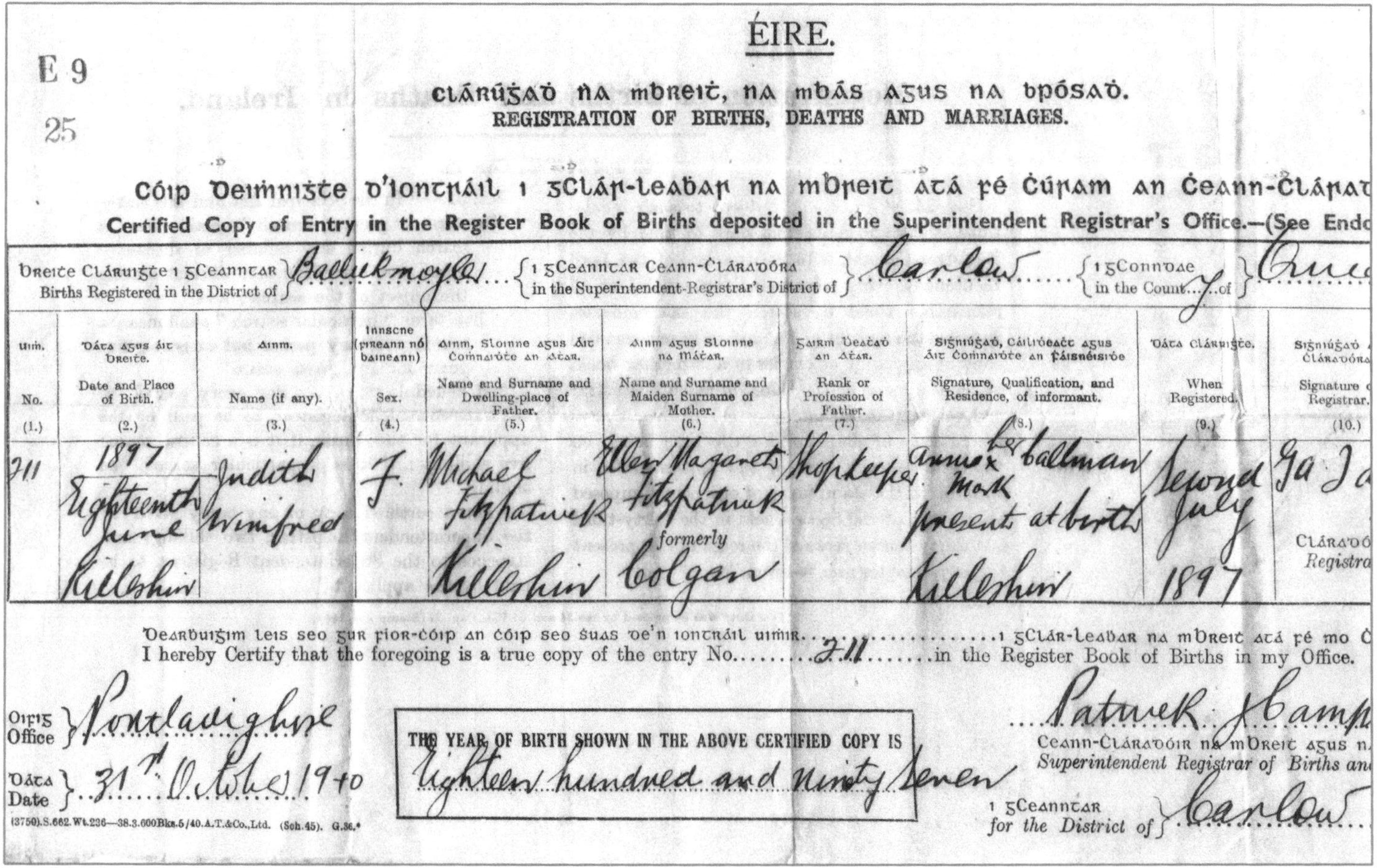

E 9

25

ÉIRE.

Cláruġaḋ na mbreiṫ, na mbás agus na bpósaḋ.
REGISTRATION OF BIRTHS, DEATHS AND MARRIAGES.

Cóip Deiṁniġṫe d'iontráil i gClár-Leabar na mBreiṫ atá fé Cúram an Ceann-Clárat
Certified Copy of Entry in the Register Book of Births deposited in the Superintendent Registrar's Office.—(See Endo

Breiṫe Cláruiġṫe i gCeanntar / Births Registered in the District of } Ballickmoyle ..... { i gCeanntar Ceann-Cláradóra / in the Superintendent-Registrar's District of } Carlow ..... { i gContae / in the County of } Carlow

Uiṁ. No. (1.)	Dáta agus áit breiṫe. Date and Place of Birth. (2.)	Ainm. Name (if any). (3.)	Inscne (fireann nó baineann) Sex. (4.)	Ainm, Sloinne agus áit Comnaiḋṫe an Aṫar. Name and Surname and Dwelling-place of Father. (5.)	Ainm agus Sloinne na Máṫar. Name and Surname and Maiden Surname of Mother. (6.)	Gairm Beaṫaḋ an Aṫar. Rank or Profession of Father. (7.)	Síniúġaḋ, Cáilíḋeaċt agus áit Comnaiḋṫe an Faisnéisiḋe. Signature, Qualification, and Residence, of informant. (8.)	Dáta Cláruiġṫe. When Registered. (9.)	Síniúġaḋ Cláradóra. Signature of Registrar. (10.)
711	1897 Eighteenth June Killeshin	Judith Winifred	F.	Michael Fitzpatrick Killeshin	Ellen Margaret Fitzpatrick formerly Colgan	Shopkeeper	Anne x Callman her mark present at birth Killeshin	Second July 1897	Ga. J. a... Cláradóir Registra...

Dearbuiġim leis seo gur fíor-cóip an cóip seo suas de'n iontráil uiṁir .... i gClár-Leabar na mBreiṫ atá fé mo C...
I hereby Certify that the foregoing is a true copy of the entry No........711........in the Register Book of Births in my Office.

Oifig / Office } Portlaoighise

Dáta / Date } 31st October 1940

THE YEAR OF BIRTH SHOWN IN THE ABOVE CERTIFIED COPY IS
Eighteen hundred and ninety seven

.....Patrick J. Camp...
Ceann-Cláradóir na mBreiṫ agus n...
Superintendent Registrar of Births an...

i gCeanntar / for the District of } Carlow

(3750).S.662.Wt.236—38.3.600Bks.5/40.A.T.&Co.,Ltd. (Sch.45). G.36.*

FIGURE 3: Pat's Birth Certificate.

FIGURE 4: Margaret (Ellen) Colgan-Fitzpatrick, Pat's Mother.

FIGURE 5: Summer life

FIGURE 6: A dapper friend of Aunt Pat's from Cannes.

FIGURE 7: Uncle Paddie & Aunt Pat dancing at a wedding.

FIGURE 8: Picnic under the trees.

FIGURE 9: Pat's Mother.

FIGURE 10: Enjoying the beach.

FIGURE 11: Pat and Kitty enjoying the Alps together.

FIGURE 12: Pat at the beach.

FIGURE 13: Pat in Clonmille.

FIGURE 14: Pat relaxing in her Paris flat.

FIGURE 15: Uncle John Colgan. Pat's sponsor.

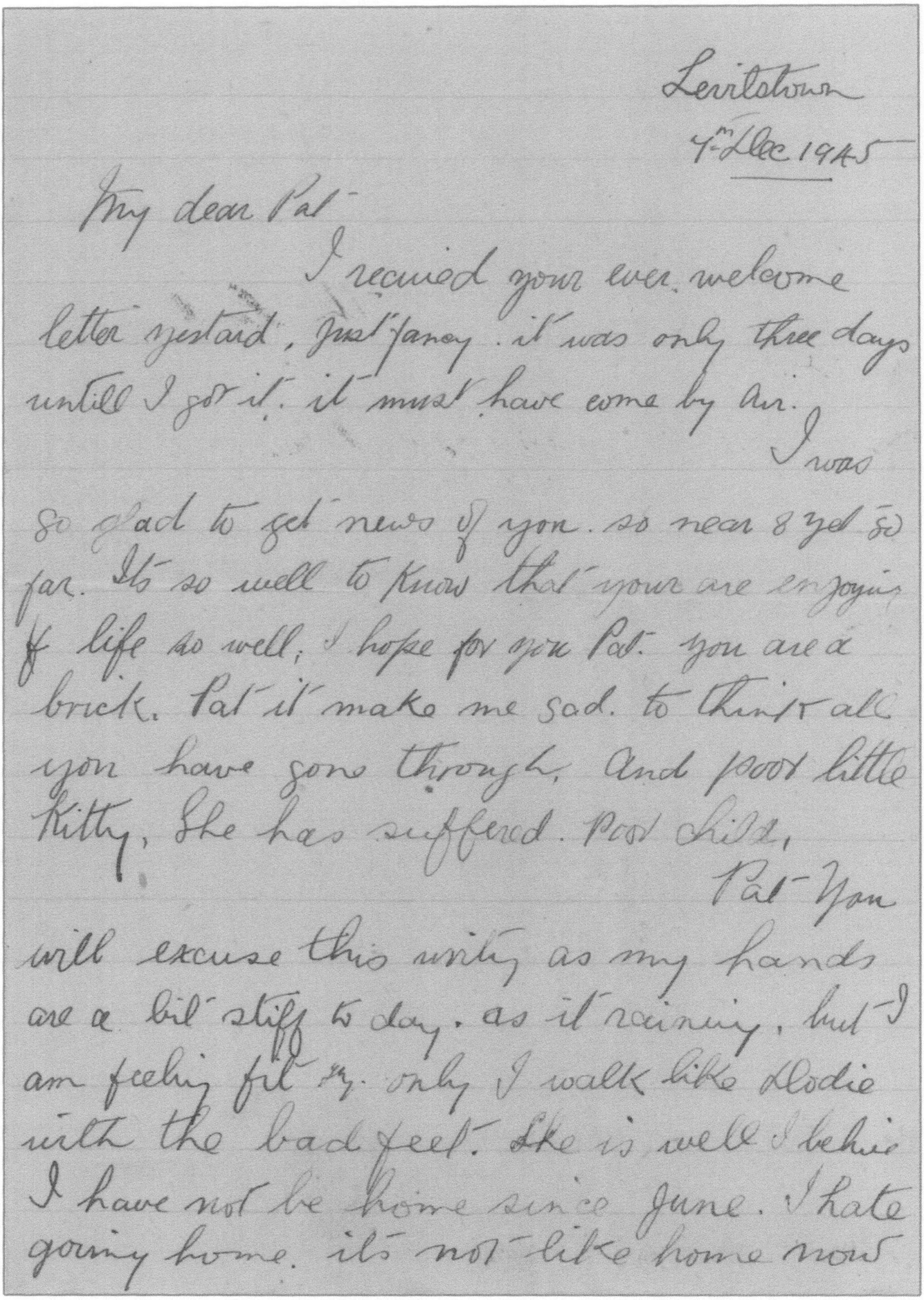

Levitstown
7th Dec 1945

My dear Pat –

I received your ever welcome letter yesterday, just fancy it was only three days untill I got it. it must have come by Air.

I was so glad to get news of you. so near & yet so far. It's so well to know that your are enjoying life so well, I hope for you Pat. you are a brick. Pat it make me sad. to think all you have gone through, And poor little Kitty, She has suffered. Poor child.

Pat You will excuse this writing as my hands are a bit stiff to day. as it raining, but I am feeling fit xy. only I walk like Dodie with the bad feet. She is well I believe I have not be home since June. I hate going home. it's not like home now

FIGURE 16A: One of two special letters. The first one awarding Pat an MBE for her work in the French Resistance. The second a letter to Pat after the war about the hardships they endured from Pat's brother Paddie and sister Schoie.

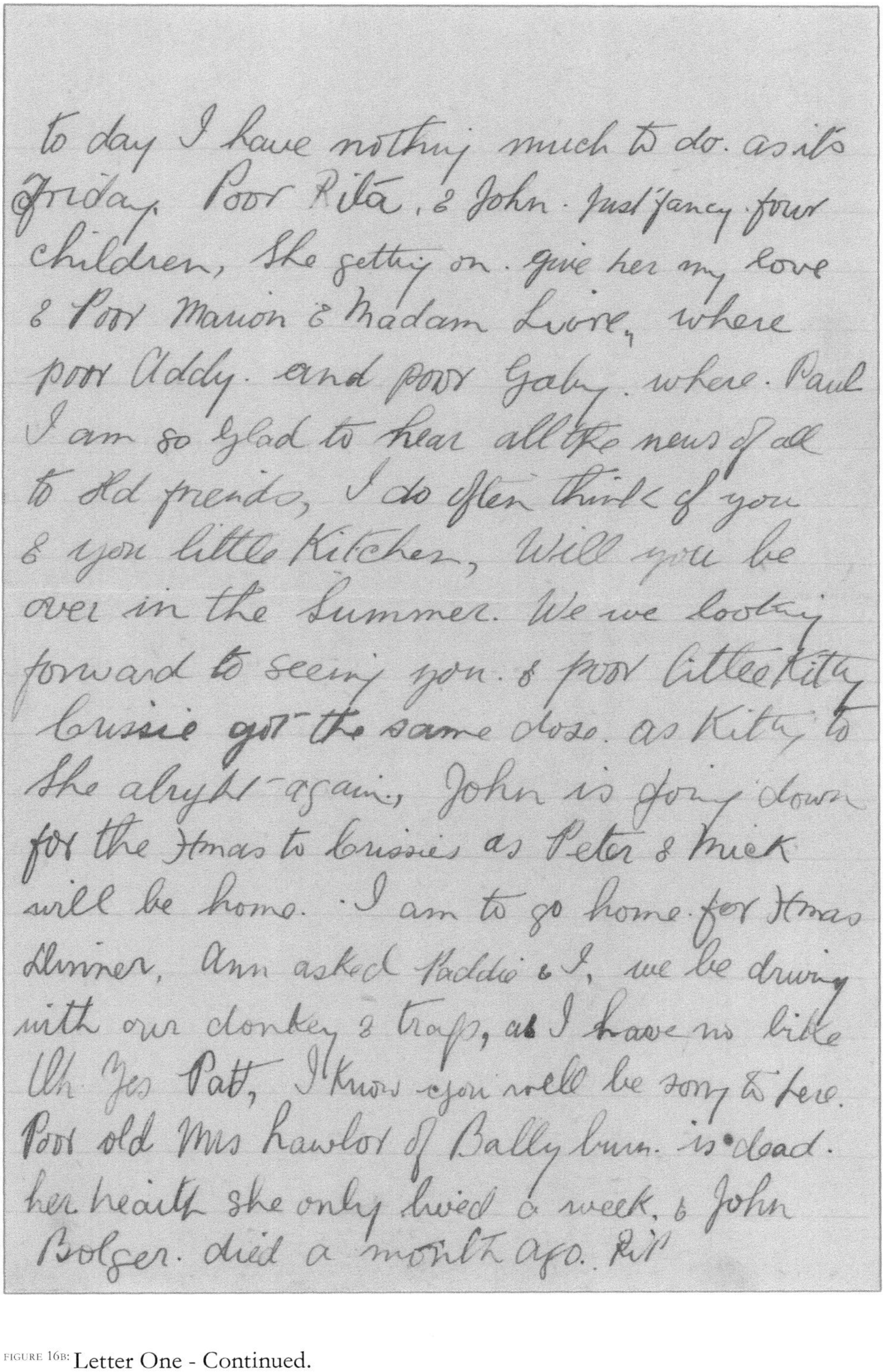

to day I have nothing much to do. as its Friday. Poor Rita, & John. Just fancy. four children, she getting on. give her my love & Poor Marion & Madam Luire, where poor Addy. and poor Gaby. where. Paul I am so glad to hear all the news of all to old friends, I do often think of you & your little Kitchen, Will you be over in the Summer. We we looking forward to seeing you. & poor little Kitty Crissie got the same dose. as Kitty to she alright again. John is going down for the Xmas to Crissies as Peter & Mick will be home. I am to go home. for Xmas dinner. Ann asked Paddie & I, we be driving with our donkey & trap, as I have no bike Uh Yes Pat, I know you well be sorry to here. Poor old Mrs Hawlor of Ballyburn. is dead. her heart she only lived a week. & John Bolger. died a month ago. Rit

FIGURE 16B: Letter One - Continued.

I want to get this Posted. So good bye. Pat. I write later. with best love.
              From Schoie & Paddie.

FIGURE 16C: Letter One - Continued.

FIGURE 17: Pat in Canne.

FIGURE 18: The Fitzpatrick family around 1904 outside their pub *'The Glenside'*. Pat Fitzpatrick is the taller girl on the right with a bow in her hair.

FIGURE 19: Kitty after Andre's murder.

FIGURE 20: Pat in uniform while in school in Belgium.

FIGURE 21: Kitty skiing.

FIGURE 22: Pat with friends in the alps.

FIGURE 23: Kitty and Andre Le Garde on their wedding day.

FIGURE 24: Pat's sister Christine my Grandmother on her wedding day to John Nelson.

FIGURE 25: Pat at the Oliver wedding.

Please Remember
in your prayers the soul of

Winifred Fitzpatrick

8, Villa Guizot, Paris

Late of Killeshin, Carlow

Who died on 2nd May, 1983

R.I.P

O Sweet Jesus, for the sake of Thy Bitter Passion and the sorrows of Thy Immaculate Mother, have mercy on her soul, and let the light of Thy Countenance shine upon her. Amen.

All I ask of you is that you will remember me at Holy Communion and at the foot of the Altar.

FIGURE 26: Aunt Pat's memorial card.

CENTRAL CHANCERY OF
THE ORDERS OF KNIGHTHOOD,
ST. JAMES'S PALACE, S.W.1.

The Secretary has the honour to transmit a Warrant of Appointment, under The King's Sign Manual, to the Most Excellent Order of the British Empire, and to request that the receipt of this Warrant may be acknowledged on the attached form.

The Secretary would be glad to receive notification of any change of permanent address, and in the event of the decease of persons holding such Warrants Executors are earnestly requested to notify the Secretary.

Miss Winifred Fitzpatrick, M.B.E.

FIGURE 27: Official letters relating to Pat's French Resistance work including her MBE award.

This certificate is awarded to

Mademoiselle Winifred Fitzpatrick

as a token of gratitude for and appreciation of the help given to the Sailors, Soldiers and Airmen of the British Commonwealth of Nations, which enabled them to escape from, or evade capture by the enemy.

Air Chief Marshal,
Deputy Supreme Commander,
Allied Expeditionary Force

1939-1945

FIGURE 28: Official letters relating to Pat's French Resistance work including her MBE award.

A touch of Killeshin in Paris

WINIFRED (Freddy) Fitzpatrick, who has died, aged 86, in Paris enjoyed the last three years of the nineteenth century growing up in Killeshin, loving every moment of it, developing an affection for home, family, neighbourhood. After a spell in Britain briefly, she lived most of her life in France. It ended some days ago in a motor accident *en route* to the south of France.

Freddy, a resolute Irishwoman lived in the very heart of Paris close to the Place de l'Etoile within a few minutes walk from the tomb of the unknown solider.

She was known to her many Paris friends as Miss Pat. She carried in her heart a love of her home hills, Killeshin, Rossmore, Bilboa, Tomard. She valued her faith, her upbringing, her family traditions.

Her maturity enabled her to move in a cosmopolitan circle of friends with ease, with dignity, with an openness to life, to novelty, to courtesy and to human need.

She taught school in France and handed on to her pupils the authentic Irish tradition which is also part of the wider European tradition of Christian living. She had a passionate attachment to the under-dog, the old pushed to the margin of life, strangers isolated in the French metropolis. She kept in touch with a wide circle of Irish friends by letters penned at all hours of the day and night. She communicated her personal concern for others widening the circle of friends by sharing with each the human concerns of all.

Freddy would wince were she to be described as a religious person. She went to the heart of Christian faith, tirelessly caring for others. She visited hospitals, calling on elderly colleagues confined to their rooms.

At 86 she expended the energy and enthusiasm more appropriate to the forties with reckless zeal. She returned to Ireland, laden with presents for all her many child friends. Only a week before her untimely death she went out to great Paris markets at Rungis to get some posters for a child in Killeshin.

Freddy returned to her native Killeshin regularly and loved to resume the contacts with her neighbours, their children and grandchildren. From Balbeg she collected fistfuls of heather for friends all over Europe.

Her zest for life was infectious. An iron will kept her on the move decades after the generality of mankind has slowed down. She saw the world, was involved in the tasks of peace and war, remained fiercely true to her loyalties. She was a vigorous, independent-minded, immensely compassionate woman. She was proud of her roots in Killeshin. She never found any good reason to abandon or to downplay the faith of her fathers, or the cultural traditions of courtesy, hospitality and welcome. As she wished, she is buried in the shadow of Holy Cross church at Killeshin. On the day we buried her the cherry was in blossom, the river was in spate, the sunshine was fitful. She is home with her own after a full, rich and generous life. She knew in whom she placed her trust. A woman of integrity. Many are grateful for the memory.

— P. J. Brophy.

FIGURE 29: This newspaper article written by P.J. Brophy describes Aunt Pat with affectionate admiration

Chapter 17

Geneva and Education, 1916

Another train journey and another change, Pat thought. She looked out the railway carriage window. That day, not even the magnificent spectacle of the rolling white landscape and the mountains with the shadows forever creeping towards evening lit by the sinking red sun touched Pat's heart. She felt as cold and as numb as though she were made of ice. The shock of Pieter's words was still rolling around her head. Whenever she closed her eyes, she could still see his beautiful face closed in with determined effort. Going through the motions to prepare for her trip had been torture. She had taken the tan leather bag out from under her bed and had started placing clothes in it only to become suddenly aware that she was standing still and that time had just disappeared. Half an hour would pass before a noise or change of light would snap her out of her trance. She just could not remember what she had been doing during that half hour. She packed and unpacked the bag until eventually, Sister Canus summoned Eve and Liza and gave them the task of packing for her.

Liza and Eve were so saddened by Pat's distress that they even tried to speak to Reverend Mother on her behalf. She firmly reminded them that their parents did not pay fees, and they were to help Pat as much as possible without interfering. The girls left the office crying and went to speak to Sister Canus, who reiterated Reverend Mother's orders and told them not to come in until the following Monday. Liza and Eve went upstairs to bid farewell to Pat. The three girls hugged and said their goodbyes. Sister Canus tried to talk to Pat but to no avail. Pat was deeply wounded, and nothing anyone could do or say was of any help. Left alone, she just waited until the time arrived for her to leave. She boarded the train with a submissive air.

When the train arrived at Geneva's main station, Pat took her bag from the shelf above her seat, buttoned her blue gabardine coat, pulled on her cream beret, and left the compartment to step down onto the platform looking around for her contact, Sister Basil. A very slim nun with black glasses stood waiting by the kiosk with a well-read daily paper under her arm. Intelligence shone from her kind eyes, and Pat knew immediately that they would get on. It turned out that Sister Basil was not that much older than Pat and for that reason had been tasked to look after her. They took a taxi to the convent, which was just five minutes down the road from the Basilica of Our Lady of Geneva. It was a small convent that could accommodate up to five sisters who were attending various educational courses in Geneva.

They arrived in the late evening, and Pat noted that the house looked unhomely, so different to the welcoming school chalets back near Bern. Switching on the bare light in the tiny kitchen only reinforced her feeling of loss. The only welcoming feature was the aroma of cooking. There was a pot of vegetable soup simmering on the cooker, which Sister Basil poured into two earthenware bowls. With few words, she placed it on the table in front of Pat along with some brown bread.

"Please do not be in a hurry to get up tomorrow morning. As it is Saturday, we have breakfast at ten a.m., which leaves us with a half hour to get to the local market," Sister Basil said gently.

Once they had finished the food, the nun showed Pat to a little room at the back of the building with a bed, wardrobe, and a chest of drawers. The curtains were drawn, and she was so exhausted that she unpacked her nightclothes, climbed into bed, and fell asleep immediately.

The next morning, she opened her eyes to see an unfamiliar pattern on the curtains in the early morning light, Pat felt that deep, sick, hopeless feeling that had been just waiting to remind her of how much she missed Pieter and how things used to be. Lying in the narrow metal bed, she felt she might as well just give up and join the nuns in their life of uncomplicated emotions and servitude. She still found it hard to believe that the gentle young man she had loved had turned into the cold person she had met that last morning, who had gone from being upset about their separation to ending their relationship with apparent single-mindedness. It just could not be.

When it was fully light, she opened the curtains and was pleasantly surprised to find that her room faced onto a small courtyard garden. In the centre was a sandstone-coloured birdbath; two little robins busily fluffed out their feathers and washed themselves with great vigour, splashing water all over the ground below. The courtyard had narrow stone paths.

Circumventing the grass along the edge of the paths were neatly trimmed miniature box hedges. Nature had the effect of calming Pat, and she couldn't wait to get dressed to explore the courtyard. It was not hard to find her way to the back door. Outside, the crisp air hit her eyes and face, giving her a sense of well-being. She loved the courtyard's small garden seats with beautiful ivy-entwined wrought-iron legs and arms and wooden-slatted seating. The seats were covered by shelters, also made from wrought iron, with very well-established winter jasmine twirling all around them.

Sitting on the bench farthest from the house, Pat allowed herself the time to just close her eyes and breathe. She was trying to control the flashbacks to Pieter's cruel words when she suddenly felt her hand being nuzzled by something cold and wet. Opening her eyes, she met the most beautiful pair of brown eyes gazing up at her. Sister Basil spoke gently, and whistling at Duke, she gestured for Pat to join her. "He is a rescue dog. The other nuns and I adore him. He is a little spoilt but so worth it."

Aunt Pat's War

She handed Pat a lead and helped her put it on the dog. Then, placing her basket over her arm, Sister Basil led the way to the Sunday market.

Chapter 18

Fewer Words Mean More

No words were spoken on the way to the Sunday market that day. Duke happily trotted along between Sister Basil and Pat. Pat was glad of the silence, which allowed her to look around and take in all the new sights. It was the kind of bright, crisp, fresh morning where the air seemed to hold onto each small sound. She was conscious of every footstep as her steamy breath led the way.

The market took place in a beautiful town square not far from the convent, with granite buildings on each side. Rows of canvas-covered stalls sold all types of produce, from cheese to wine to bags made of goat and calfskin. It was beautifully neat and clean, and the smells that emanated from the different stalls were new and captivating. Duke was very interested in the food stalls, especially those that sold Swiss sausage. He had to be hauled back from going under the meat counter as he attempted to scavenge even the smallest morsel.

"Mademoiselle, un Cadeau!" Farmers plying their produce offered samples.

As Pat tasted a fresh piece of homemade chocolate, she noticed that everyone here spoke French, unlike Bern, where it was a mix of French and German. She delighted in being able to listen in on the different conversations. Sister Basil was fluent, and soon her shopping list was complete, in her basket, and covered in a muslin cloth.

"Pat, there is someone I would like you to meet. He has invited us to drop in for a cup of tea. He is a professor of linguistics at the University of Geneva, and I have been in touch with him to oversee your studies while you are here."

"That's great," said Pat, though she really couldn't care less as she examined a stall selling different types of jams, jellies, and conserves.

As they came to the end of the market and were about to head back to the house to drop off the basket before heading for tea, she noticed a little old lady dressed in traditional Swiss clothes. She was sitting behind a low table covered in the most delicate pieces of lace. Pat could not resist. She bought a lace trim suitable to make into a collar for her Sunday best dress. As she paid, the old woman suddenly grabbed Pat's hand; turning it, she drew a finger along her lifeline. "Mademoiselle, you will live a long and exciting life," the old woman exclaimed, "but you will never marry or bear children. You are so brave."

Seeing the shock on Pat's face, Sister Basil pulled her away by the arm. Pat did not have time to think about these words until much later—she was struggling to keep up with the very agitated nun. Making a quick detour to drop their purchases off at the house, they arrived dogless and basketless at Professor Gironet's rooms at the university. "Bonjour," a man in his fifties greeted them with a polite bow. He ushered them into his sitting-room, seated them by the welcoming fire, and went to arrange for his assistant-cum-housekeeper to bring tea. After a while, a neat, graceful young man appeared, and with an almost theatrical flourish, he placed a large tray on the low coffee table before the fire. The four of them sat together.

"Basil tells me that you are a competent student, Pat. She also tells me that your languages are superb. I am so looking forward to working with you. This is my assistant, Piero, my right-hand man." Professor

Gironet nodded at Piero, who clasped his neat hands to his chest and shyly looked at Pat. She could not help but smile at the two of them, as they were so sweet and interesting. "Thank you, Professor and Piero. I look forward to working with you also," she said, surprised that she meant it.

Two hours passed so quickly that when the carriage clock chimed 5:30 p.m., Sister Basil jumped up and told Pat that they needed to leave immediately as the other nuns were preparing a meal to welcome her to Geneva. They said a very hurried but warm goodbye and arranged that Pat would call at Professor Gironet's rooms at ten sharp the following morning to begin her lessons.

Something was niggling away in Pat's mind as she walked swiftly back to the house. It was an emotion that she did not want to acknowledge, but to her surprise, it just came to her. She felt happy. *Yes, but only a little bit,* she thought.

As they entered the little courtyard, Duke shot through the kitchen door, emitting a welcoming bark. Having washed her hands and combed her hair, Pat returned to the kitchen, where bowls of steaming beef stroganoff and baked potatoes were waiting on the kitchen table. *These nuns are dressed very casually*, Pat thought. They wore dark-coloured skirts and white or cream blouses. Woollen cardigans seemed very much in favour with these women.

Sister Basil sat at the head of the table and led the conversation, which jumped from college news to the war and then to her beloved Duke. She intermittently asked Pat about her family and Langerbrugge. These learned ladies treating her as an equal was irresistible, and Pat was soon chatting away. The nuns were fascinated that she had travelled to Belgium at age eleven, mostly alone, and how she had adjusted to a new life. Switching to French, she was well able to keep up, and their compliments about her ability and her accent delighted her.

Sister Basil took a large apple tart from the oven and placed a jug of cream on the table. "Welcome, Miss Pat. We wish you a happy and interesting stay in Geneva. Feel free to ask us anything. Sisters Marie, Jeanette, Teresa, and Magda are at the college most days, but we always eat together in the evening. So, anything at all, just ask. We have all, at one stage, been new to Geneva, and we love to share our affection for this beautiful city."

Chapter 19

Culture and Freedom

The Professor declared a 'culture week'—a week dedicated to Pat's higher education, enlightenment, and entertainment.

The two men spent the evening after their return from the Musée Ariana planning a full and varied itinerary covering everything they could think of to make Pat feel as though life had become a whirlwind of interesting people, beautiful places, and artworks. She was spending very little time at the house, or 'Cabane d'oiseaux' (the birdhouse) as Professor and Piero called it, a joking reference to six women living together. She would arrive home late, around ten thirty, to find the lights off and everybody in their rooms preparing for the next day. There was always a cheerful "Goodnight!" with no questions asked. Pat thought nothing of it, as she was usually too tired. She would just give Duke a quick rub and rush up to bed to dream amazing dreams—in French, of course.

By Wednesday of that week, they had visited nearly all the major attractions and gardens and had tasted an array of foods both local and exotic, all of which Pat relished, especially the fare at the famous La Maison du Chocolat. She grew accustomed to sparkling prosecco at lunch and a good glass of claret at dinner. Professor refused to allow her to question whether or not she should be having alcohol: "Mademoiselle

Aunt Pat's War

Pat, it is part of your integration into a natural and beautiful Swiss-French life." It just took one little glass before she became so giggly and happy that all she could do was smile in agreement. Her world began and ended with Professor and Piero; she had neither time nor energy for anything else. Even poor Duke looked at her with doleful eyes as she returned late every evening. But she could not control herself—she wanted to stay out later and later. For the first time in her life, she felt grown-up and completely alive.

One evening, realising she had not thought about Pieter for ages, she finally acknowledged that she was over him. The next morning, walking into the professor's sitting room, she was surprised to see a tall lady with short hair framing her beautiful face and large eyes. She was dressed in what appeared to Pat to be the height of fashion, at least, according to the magazines she read. Her hemline was at least five if not ten inches shorter than Pat's. Pat was fascinated.

Professor introduced the tall woman as his cousin, Letitia. Pat felt her gut tingle. For some reason, she did not find the professor's introduction entirely convincing. "Bonjour, Mademoiselle Pat, lovely to meet you at last. My darling cousin has asked me to take you shopping," Letitia purred as she air-kissed Pat on either cheek, leaving a scent of rose water with almond combined with just a hint of tobacco.

Pat could hardly reply, so transfixed was she by Letitia's pursed and pouty red lips. Piero, realising that Pat was a little overwhelmed, quickly came to the rescue. "I know that Pat will just adore your plan, as I am sure any girl would. Isn't that correct, Pat?"

"Oh, yes," Pat stammered, and she allowed Letitia to lead her toward the tram.

Mimsie was a shop unlike any other Pat had ever been in. It was a salon for ladies, Letitia explained. The models would show outfits that the owner, Mademoiselle Mimsie, felt would suit the client. Once the client had chosen various items, her staff would bring the garments to a private fitting room. It was such fun. The most elegant and stylish ladies paraded up and down the floor in front of Letitia and Pat, sweeping around and out through the curtains to reappear a short time later wearing an entirely different outfit. The attendants handed Letitia and Pat glasses of champagne even though it was only noon and served them a little dish of biscuits and chocolate to nibble on. Pat tried not to fidget. She was mesmerised by her companion's poise and worldliness. Letitia came from a different dimension, so unlike Pat's world. Pat had never met anyone like her. It was true that she had spent a lot of time with strong women, but they were almost exclusively religious or academic—nothing like Letitia.

"What do you think, dear Pat, is this not exciting? And now for the undergarments."

Letitia arranged for an attendant to take Pat's measurements in a small, curtained area at the back of the salon. Once the fitter was finished and had gone to check her stock, Letitia peeped through the fitting-room curtain as Pat stood there in her old school slip. Letitia let out a screech. "Oh my god, Miss Pat—your legs and underarms are like those of an animal! Why do you not shave? We shall fix this next."

Pat could only utter a perplexed "Eh?" as she had no idea what Letitia was going on about.

Once they had finished in Mimsie, Pat grasped a large paper bag with the silhouette of a fashionable lady posing under the boutique's name in gold letters. She was a little confused as the bag felt very light considering all the clothes she had tried on. Waving goodbye to Mademoiselle, Letitia linked her arm with Pat's and whispered, "My dressmaker will copy all those magnificent dresses, don't you worry; only your new underwear is in the bag. But now we have a very important purchase to make."

First, they bought some Poudre Subtile depilatory cream in the local chemist and then ordered a lady's razor, to be collected the following week. This led to Pat owning one of the most popular fashion items available, the Gillette Milady Décolleté ladies' shaver. She tried it out for the first time alone in her little bedroom lest one of the nuns see it. She ended with patches of blood in places where she had exerted too much pressure, but despite that, she felt really sophisticated, pain or no pain. Little did she know that Sister Basil had conspired with Professor, Piero, and Letitia to orchestrate the entire experience, and she was very pleased with the results.

Chapter 20

For the Best

The screech of brakes as the tram stopped outside La Maison tea rooms jolted Pat from her thoughts. That morning, she had received a letter forwarded from Bern. It was a letter from Killeshin with plenty of news about the family. Mother had been very unwell and was now unable to walk. She needed to be carried downstairs in the morning and upstairs at night. This meant that Christine and the girls were doing most of the chores; Paddy and John were helping Father in the pub and on the farm. Christine's description of the family gathering the previous Sunday evening made Pat homesick. She could imagine Christine playing the squeezebox and the sound of feet tapping. The younger ones would get more and more excited until Scholastica (known as Sco), Gertie, and Kitty would have to jump up and jig around the floor, swinging each other round and round until Mother would cry, "You will be sick, enough, enough!" while at the same time laughing at the giddy energy of her girls. Father would be by the heaped fire in the parlour, pipe hanging from his mouth as he sipped a small shot of whiskey. The loss of Pieter had ignited a feeling of loneliness in Pat that she was finding hard to shake off. Now the letter from home with its warm, loving descriptions made her feel she just wanted to be at home in Killeshin, where life did not seem so cruel.

She had started her studies with Professor Gironet and was getting used to travelling on her own to and from his rooms. She loved the classes. Professor and Piero were like a comedy act, and the lessons were filled with laughter and fun. Their banter was relaxed and amusing. They conversed in French and at such a pace that it took Pat a few days to fully decipher what they were saying. However, her French was of such a high standard that by the second week, she was able to add her own comments to the repartée. Then Piero would insist that they speak in English, as he wanted to pass his oral English exam in the college at the end of the year. Pat had never spent time with men before, other than with her father and brothers and of course, Pieter. She found the professor and Piero to be very different. They were well-educated and read voraciously. The conversation would switch from literature to music to history, and great arguments constantly erupted between them about politics and the war.

One particular morning, as she travelled by tram to college, she began to think about all these things, and in particular, how she should be grateful for her new independent life. And yet…

A whistling Professor Gironet opened the door to Pat that morning and looked at her from under his bushy eyebrows with concern. "Ah, Miss Pat. Today, I have a new plan. Do not take off your coat. We are going to practise your French in town. Come Piero, we are going out."

"But Monsieur, what about the schedule?" whinged Piero.

Grabbing Pat by the arm and throwing on his tweed overcoat and Russian-style fur hat, the normally jovial professor growled, "We are going now, Piero." Piero had no choice but to pull his overcoat and hat from the hall stand and follow them out and down the red and black tiled path. This day would stand out in Pat's mind forever, such was the fun they had. Years later, the professor would tell her that the sight of her sad face that morning had motivated him to change his plan, and the schedule be damned.

The tram stopped outside Musée du Petit Palais. It was a beautiful, tall, granite building that housed a wonderful collection of paintings and sculptures. Professor took Pat by the arm, and Piero straggled behind them up the stone steps. The atmosphere was reverent except for the suppressed whispers of a group ahead of them. Professor led Pat through the magnificent mahogany double doors, where a waft of lavender-scented polish greeted them. Pat had been to museums and art galleries before but never with such an eager and knowledgeable guide. Professor insisted on leaving their coats in the cloakroom. She could feel his excitement as he led her into the first exhibition room. The room was filled with works by the Russian artist Nicholas Tarkhoff. She loved his pictures, so full of colour. She related to many of the subjects such as "Cat with Child", which reminded her of Tabby, the barn cat at home. Room after room of thought-provoking art filled her with a thirst for information on the artists and their lives. Pat developed a fascination for art she would enjoy for the rest of her life. She was engrossed, and only when Piero refused to move another step until they had lunch did she realise that she was starving—yes, starving. Silent with tiredness and swamped with information, they collected their coats and took the tram to La Maison. There was no question as to what they were having to eat. They just sat down at a lovely little table by the large front window. Soon, three plates of goulash, a basket of fresh white bread covered in a white napkin, three glasses of water, and a flute each of sparkling wine were placed in front of them. The only sound was the occasional "Mmm!" as they savoured each mouthful of their meal. Pulling the bread apart and soaking up the last of the juice on his plate, Professor Gironet raised his glass of wine and toasted, "To Miss Pat, whose life is only just beginning. Laughter, music, and love."

Brushing away her protest that she might not be allowed wine so early in the day, he clinked his glass with hers. She didn't know if it was the rising bubbles or the company, but Pat felt a definite sense of optimism.

Aunt Pat's War

1916 rolled into 1917 in a whirl of multicoloured silk, satin, and chiffon. Anyone who met Pat for the first time then would have thought her only problem might be what shoes to choose to match her outfits.

Earlier, before she returned to Ireland for a visit in the summer of 1916, however, Pat had heard about a rising in Dublin at Easter of that year. The country was unsettled and divided. Between the war in Europe and trouble in Ireland, she had been very lucky to make it home for a month that summer. She could not relax fully until she reached Killeshin. Her arrival had met with great excitement. She brought bags of clothes that she had collected from various wealthy contacts. She divided the clothes between her sisters. They tried on every item, parading up and down the parlour, deciding which outfits suited which sister or how they could adjust them to fit. Pat and the girls spent each evening sewing and chatting together, and she told them all about her exciting life. Using her exceptional mimicry skills, she sent them into convulsions of laughter. Pat saw her home through changed eyes.

Chapter 21

Dancing Shoes

Clink, clink. "Cheers!"

Holding the slim stem of her champagne glass in one hand and a cheroot in the other, Pat nearly choked after a deep inhalation of tobacco smoke while trying to look as if she had been smoking for a long time. Quickly gulping down some champagne, she could not help but roar with laughter as she watched Piero and one of her friends awkwardly twirling across the pale blond parquet dance floor of the Hotel Geneva.

It was 18 June 1917, and it was Pat's twentieth birthday party. She was in higher spirits than any champagne could ever make her, and she looked it. Once Letitia had taken her under her wing the previous year, Pat had become a most attractive, well-groomed, modern young woman. Professor had organised some of his best college students into a conversation group, which met three times a week at his home. He soon discovered that Pat's language ability was equal if not superior to that of the other students and had adjusted her assignments accordingly. Now, no one spoke English at all at the professor's. Poor Piero had to beg Pat to meet him for coffee and conversation twice a week, which she insisted he repay by accompanying her to dancing lessons at the Hotel Geneva every Tuesday evening.

Madame Sophie was a French lady who had married a man from Geneva, and in response to popular demand, she had set up a dance studio. She taught all types of dance—ballet, waltz, and even the Charleston, which was very popular. Madame Sophie had lived in New York for a year and had seen first-hand the arrival of the famous dance from the Deep South on the Harlem stage. She was the first to introduce it to Geneva, and subsequently, she had developed a very well-attended dance salon popular with all ages. These Tuesday evening classes were great fun, and through them, Pat and Piero received invitations to various tea dances and parties. Life was exciting, and Letitia made sure that Pat was not only suitably attired but also kept to designated curfews that Sister Basil insisted upon. Above all, Pat's formal education came first, and there was no way anything could interfere with that.

For some time, Pat's aunt's and uncle's letters made her aware that if she thought one of her sisters had the potential to make a life for herself with Pat, they would support her decision and make appropriate arrangements. Christine ran the home now, and the only sister who was suitable was Kitty, a bright, cheerful soul who was quick to learn and very sociable. During one of Pat's visits home, her parents decided that after Christmas, Kitty would travel with Pat to France to open an English-speaking guesthouse for paying guests in Normandy. These had become very popular in that region, and Pat's ability to tutor private pupils in both English and French would generate more income. Kitty was a hard worker, as well, and a very quick learner. Pat was confident that Kitty would thrive given such an opportunity. There was talk of nothing else that holiday.

As the last day of Pat's visit loomed, she and Christine walked up Killeshin Hill to spend some time alone together. A warm, gentle breeze whistled around them. But between the sisters, there was silence for quite some time. Being up there was beyond words. So many memories, sad and happy, wrapped around them as they sat on the green verges of their family graves. Christine felt sad about being left behind, but she assured Pat that she could never leave Co Laois and the younger siblings. She was happy for both Pat and Kitty and made light of it by joking that next time Pat came home, she wanted a bigger share of the clothes. Arms around each other's waists, they climbed down the hill and never spoke about that afternoon again.

That evening, teatime in the cosy parlour was full of chat and laughter. There was a special treat of beef bought in town and cooked slowly in the Aga, together with crispy roast potatoes and peas picked from the back garden. Freshly baked apple tart and cream completed a meal that would live on in Pat's taste buds for a long time to come.

Finally, the family knelt facing their chairs to say the rosary. Once the five Sorrowful Mysteries were over, Pat started to rise from her knees, but a glare from Father stopped her. She plonked herself quickly back down to continue with the Memorare, where she remained until she saw her father rise stiffly to his feet.

Pat had taken the opportunity during that holiday to travel to England to visit her friends the Goodrums, whom she had met through Aunt Ada. This had given her family in Killeshin time to adjust to Kitty's imminent departure. Saying goodbye to loved ones had never been easy for Pat, but now she was so determined to make sure that Kitty was all right that she could not dwell on her own feelings. Once they had waved goodbye to the family, Pat allowed herself to enjoy having Kitty with her. She was such a bright spirit who looked forward to every little detail of her new life in France. They would never forget the voyage from Ireland to Geneva. Many boats and trains later, they finally arrived. Pat knew this would probably be her last such trip, as they would be based in Normandy shortly.

Chapter 22

Time to Move On

Snapping the trunk shut, the porter placed it and the other smaller cases onto the Paris train. Pat had said a very sad goodbye to Geneva and all her wonderful friends with a heavy heart. It seemed like an eternity ago instead of just a couple of months. Professor Gironet assured her that this was the perfect time to make a fresh start, and they would all visit her once she had settled into her new life. The war was over, and she was a competent tutor. They held a wonderful afternoon tea party in the professor's rooms. Pat had been deeply moved by the warm send-off. She promised to stay in touch, making sure that they had all written a message in her autograph book. Many tears later and she left Geneva a totally different person to the one who had arrived there. This time she was not alone but had Kitty by her side. They departed Geneva at the end of November, and although Pat was well used to travelling, for some reason, this trip felt surreal.

"How long will it take, Pat?" asked Kitty, squeezing her arm. Yes, this time it was different, Pat realised. Now she had the responsibility of looking after her sister. Before this, and for such a long time, she had only had herself to think about; although she was thrilled to have Kitty living with her, it would take some adjustment. They arrived in Paris some hours later, where they were to stay overnight. They had an appointment with Monsieur Renard, a notary, about Pat's affairs the following morning. They stayed with Sister Bernarde, a contact of Sister Basil's, near the train station as they did not want to haul their baggage too far. The following morning, Kitty was up at dawn, looking out the window and trying to catch even a glimpse of the famous Paris. There was nothing Pat could do but eat breakfast quickly and take her sister for a walk. Kitty was enraptured and squeezed her guide every two minutes in delight.

They just about made their nine a.m. appointment with Monsieur Renard. He appeared to be in a great hurry to conclude their meeting, but just as they were ready to leave, he beckoned Pat aside. He quietly advised her to buy first-class train tickets to Normandy to avoid the wounded and distraught soldiers at the station who were still returning from battlefields as far away as East Africa. He felt it might be too upsetting for "Petite Kitty".

The lilting sound of a lone mouth organ playing "Roses Are Shining in Picardy" greeted them as they walked into the train station. The Great War had been over for six months now, but the station was still filled with soldiers from all over the world. Many had been in prisoner-of-war-camps, and nearly all looked pitiful. One group was in such bad shape, it was obvious they would never live any type of normal life again. Bewilderment was etched on the faces of even those soldiers who looked physically well. It was extremely upsetting for Pat to see this, but she kept telling Kitty all about the fantastic plans she had, trying to distract her sister from the terrible sights surrounding her. She was relieved that teenage Kitty seemed so excited about living in a villa in Normandy that she was almost oblivious to everything else.

Through the Goodrum's great friends, the Schnerb family, Pat had acquired an eight-bedroom villa facing the sea with its own lawn tennis court. She had a photograph of the villa, and Kitty kept asking if she could see it. She had never seen such a house and was trying to conjure up some of the French words that Pat had instructed her to use when showing delight, "La villa c'est gros," stuttered Kitty.

Pat, delighted with the effort and to keep Kitty occupied, replied, "Non, la villa est grande. Brava, Kitty—intelligente."

Upon hearing the whistle for their train's departure, Pat took Kitty by the arm and led her into their very plush compartment. It was well worth the extra money. The compartment had magnificent red velvet seats with antique cream tassels on lace headrests. There was a waiter service, which Pat promised Kitty she could use by pressing a brass bell in the wall between the windows once they were an hour outside Paris.

What company Kitty was! She saw everything as new, sometimes reacting with elated screeches. It was a memorable journey for them both. Kitty often spoke to Pat about it over the following years. She was innocent, having never travelled before. She was bubbling with excitement, so much so that about a half an hour into the train journey, she fell fast asleep mid-sentence with her head on Pat's shoulder. This gave Pat time to think about all the poor soldiers she had seen in Paris. It brought her mind back to Pieter. She had returned to Bern only once from Geneva. Professor Gironet and Sister Basil had made the decision that she had outgrown college. She went back to Bern to collect some things she had left there and to say goodbye to the nuns and students properly. She had left in a flurry of upset, and it had taken her all this time to see the wisdom of their decision to send her to Geneva. Pat was in her twenties and ready to move forward with her life. The plan to open her own guest house and tutor students was well in place. She felt she only had one piece of unfinished business to attend to in Bern—Pieter.

Taking that walk over the mountain path to his house was very difficult, but something drove her forward. Arriving at the little chalet, she could see a light coming from the barn. At one stage, she nearly turned back, but just then, out he came, face to face with her, and it was too late. Dropping a pail of milk in shock, he walked quickly towards her and took her in his arms, muttering, "Mon Pat, mon Pat. How different you look. More beautiful. I have dreamt of this moment for so long, and now here you are. Forgive me, please. I had to appear so cruel, had to let you go."

Pat was having none of it. Looking around her slowly, she pushed him away. "You lied to me. I would have waited for you. I thought we could speak about anything, and you were so harsh and cold and gave no warning. I would never take you back. Never. Remember that it was your fault, and you have to live with it."

With that, she left without looking back. A shiver ran down her spine as she remembered the fortune-teller's words, "You will never marry, and you will never have children."

Back straight, shoulders squared, and nose in the air, she thought, *So be it. At least my life will be exciting.*

The train slowed and pulled into the station with a cloud of steam. Pat gently shook Kitty awake, and they prepared to gather their luggage. Under her breath, Kitty constantly hummed the same little song. Pat couldn't help but become as excited as her sister. She, too, began seeing the future through new eyes.

Chapter 23

Villiers-sur-Mer

"English Home"—the words stood out in large black capitals on the front page of the Deauville and Villiers-sur-Mer newspaper. Pat and Kitty admired the advertisement they had placed for their new guesthouse. They read the ad out loud repeatedly as they walked back from the village, using different accents and ranges of tone and making funny faces to match each character's voice. Returning from the post office and shops where they had placed buff-coloured cards containing the same advertisement, they stood and admired Villa Durenne and its long front garden, at the end of which was a little pebbled path, trimmed with scallop-shaped cement tiles mixed with seashells. It was a welcoming house, with its two-storey bay windows on either side and an impressive cream and blue wooden porch with a grey slate roof.

Pat had insisted that they find as many deep red geranium plants as possible, and with a nod to the beauty of Switzerland, she placed them on either side of the front door. They had been in Normandy for a month, and in that time they worked alongside a cleaning lady, Hélène, and her husband Marc, an odd job man, to transform the villa into a most charming, comfortable home. Before Pat took over the Villa Durenne, two old ladies ran it as a boarding house for many years. The old ladies had retired when the previous season had finished. It was an advantage that the name was already known, and the furniture was included as part of the sale for a small fee. Pat had felt it was a promising purchase.

They had attacked the eight bedrooms, first throwing open the windows and taking down the curtains. They rolled up the rugs and took them out to the back, hung them on the washing line, and beat them with carpet beaters to get rid of dirt and grime. Pat took a moment to admire the view of the ever-changing sea. Strong sunshine seemed to throw diamonds in the air as waves rolled towards the beach. She stood with a pile of towels in her arms, deeply inhaling the salty air coming up from the beach while acknowledging how lucky she was.

That evening, after a heavy day cleaning and sorting through all the old bed linen and blankets, the two sisters could hardly summon the energy to eat and had gone to bed in their shared bedroom exhausted, only to be awakened by an unbearable need to scratch themselves all over. Even their tiredness would not allow them to go back to sleep. Unable to take it any longer, they had turned on the brightest light in the room to find that the mattress, which had been part of the sale, was infested with families of bedbugs, very happily tangoing away after what appeared to be many years of practise. Pulling their dressing gowns on, Kitty and Pat made their way downstairs to try to get some sleep on the sofa in the sitting room. They decided to deal with the bedbug problem the following morning. Even then, neither Pat nor Kitty got much sleep, as when one stopped scratching, the other would start. In the end, they just accepted that a light snooze was the best rest they would get that night. Kitty finally dropped off into a deep sleep around six a.m. She awoke three hours later when she heard Pat shouting from upstairs—French words that Kitty had not yet heard but guessed the meaning of, "Merde! Merde, dégoûtant petits bâtards!"

Pat had just finished pulling all the mattresses from each bedroom and was about to hurl them down the stairs one at a time. She could not bear it. She had discovered that the bedbugs were not confined to one mattress. No, all the mattresses were infested with the "dégoûtant bâtards". Kitty got up immediately and, still in her pyjamas, helped Pat, Hélène, and Marc drag and pull the heavy horsehair mattresses out to the backyard. Marc instructed them to wait while he fetched some chopped wood from the woodpile and some old newspapers from the kitchen to place between them. The pile reached quite a height. They decided to light a huge bonfire that very evening, and along with the mattresses, burn some pieces of furniture that were so chewed up by woodworm that not even the French—who considered woodworm a sign of antiquity—thought them worth saving.

Pat and Kitty dragged themselves around all day, trying to work as hard as they could at cleaning all the surfaces around the beds with white vinegar and warm water. Any fabric, including tablecloths and doilies, that might have even touched the beds was taken downstairs to the scullery to be boiled and washed over the following days. Soon, the villa smelled of carbolic soap and white vinegar. The steam coming from the scullery seemed to create a continuous sauna-like atmosphere. For the evening meal, Hélène baked quiche and served it with fresh bread and a small tumbler of red wine for each of them. They decided to eat their meal outdoors.

Hélène set up a picnic on the trestle table in the yard and covered the food in gingham napkins until they were ready. They ate silently, gulping down their meal as they realised that they had not had time to eat all day. Standing beside Marc as he prepared the fire, Pat thought she had never seen such tired, scruffy faces. He poured petrol over the great pile of mattresses and wood and handed her a pile of curled newspapers lit by a match, which she immediately threw on the heap. The pile was so dry and well-prepared that it ignited in seconds, causing them to all pull back quickly, watching silently as the fire took hold.

Looking on as the golden and crimson flames licked the dry wood and paper, Pat felt at peace. She had a home, a career, independence, but most important of all, she now had her sister Kitty—a part of Killeshin to fill the loneliness she had experienced since she left home. Life had never been better. Staring up at the starlit sky, they clinked tumblers and chanted, "À votre santé." Pat and Kitty linked arms as each thought deep thoughts about life and all its changes and meanings.

Chapter 24

Villa Durenne to Paris

Les Années Folles, the "Crazy Years", swept through France once the terrible First World War ended. No war had ever before affected or disrupted so many people across Europe. The surge of optimism for a new start aroused a desire in everyone not only to work hard but to play hard too.

Villa Durenne embraced every opportunity this new world offered. Pat and Kitty quickly made a lot of new friends in Villiers-sur-Mer and settled into a happy and fulfilled life. The summers were filled with organising guests and everything that went with it.

At first, after they opened, there were many very tense moments. It took ages to fully judge the amount of food and other items required to run a successful boarding house. In their later years, the previous owners had slowed the business down, only taking in guests they knew and on a long-term basis, so Kitty and Pat had to learn a lot themselves through trial and error. Jack Goodrum was a frequent visitor, and with his help, they cleared out the yard and tidied up the gardens. He helped to cultivate the lawn and marked it out for guests to play games of lawn tennis and croquet. Picnics and swimming parties at the beach proved to be most popular. Pat paid particular attention to the quality and quantity of food provided in the wicker picnic baskets with their bright red and white napkins. The beach ponies benefited from these picnic baskets greatly. Often, children of the guests fed them leftover apple cores, the ponies nuzzling their hands with their hairy mouths.

There was something for everyone at Villa Durenne—good food, company, entertainment, plenty of outdoor activities, and just a sense of a place where people could relax and have their needs well catered to. Kitty grew up quickly, becoming a petite, pretty young lady with beautiful rich brunette hair. She and Pat remained very close, something that brought great contentment to Pat, as she felt that she had a piece of home with her at all times.

The post had improved greatly since the end of the war, so they wrote and received many letters, especially from Ireland. In Killeshin, Kitty's letters proved most popular as she wrote entertaining and amusing stories about the guests and her happy life.

Pat developed a keen interest in the suffragette movement, which she followed very closely. She had hoped that once the war was over, the French government would bring in votes for women. However, like many other women of that time, she was left frustrated—so much effort made with only broken promises to show for it. By 1918, in Ireland and the UK, women could vote only at the age of thirty, and then only if they met certain requirements. 1922 was a very progressive year, when the Irish Free State introduced votes for women. This coincided with the explosion of radio into the world. Maurice Chevalier became a household name, and it seemed as if he had created clones of himself, as so many men emulated not only his look but also his charming manner. "Dans la vie faut pas s'en faire" or "Then There Is Nothing to Worry About", released in 1921, became a firm favourite with everyone at Villa Durenne. Pat purchased a radio in 1922, and Mademoiselle Brodeur, a guest, would play the piano along to Maurice Chevalier with everyone joining in the chorus. This routine became a perfect ending to many a busy but happy holiday.

"Godfathers, Kitty! The nuns want to come to stay for a week in September," Pat announced one day in early August. Kitty could not see the problem, but Pat led such a relaxed and independent life now, she never wanted things to revert. She and Jack Goodrum had become extremely close; he was due from England the same week as the nuns' proposed visit, and this was causing her concern. In true Pat fashion, she set about organising the best week that anyone could possibly give three nuns in their seventies, making sure that their rooms were on the ground level and that the beds were comfortable and not too high off the floor. She was fully prepared for what she thought would by now be three extremely geriatric ladies, as she hadn't seen them for some time. That Tuesday, Jack arrived first, and she decided to bring him with her to collect the sisters from the station at seven p.m. Wow! Much to her surprise and Jack's amusement, three upright, sprightly ladies descended from the train. None was wearing religious garb. Instead, the three nuns wore bright, summery clothing and sported large straw hats. Gathering their bags, they set off back to Villa Durenne, full of chat and news from Switzerland. The professor and Piero had sent their best wishes and promised to visit the following spring. It was all Pat could do to stop herself from roaring with laughter as she caught Jack's amused look in the rear-view mirror of the Citroën.

The nuns were thrilled to meet Kitty at last, and she immediately took to making them as comfortable as possible while Pat went to tell Hélène that they would have dinner in ten minutes. They loved Jack and were genuinely delighted to see that Pat had met such a nice man from such a decent family. They knew the Goodrums through Ada and John Colgan. They had great fun that evening, remembering the many stories from Langerbrugge and Bern, especially how the eleven-year-old Pat had arrived from Ireland with no French and had mastered the language in such a short time through pig-headed determination. They recalled how at first, she had found it so difficult to fit in before then becoming the ringleader of many a prank as well as the orchestrator of memorable Christmas and Easter plays.

Aunt Pat's War

Kitty drank in every word. She was itching to write a long letter home to Christine telling her exactly what Pat had got up to in college so many years ago. It had been a frequent mealtime topic in Killeshin for most of her childhood. Now at last she knew what really happened, and she could not wait to share it.

Chapter 25

Guests at Villa Durenne

Piano music drifted out through the open parlour window as Kitty practised with Mademoiselle Brodeur. Mademoiselle had been a long-term paying guest at the villa for three years now, and she gave Kitty lessons in exchange for a reduction in her rent. A retired teacher, she was a gentle lady from Bordeaux who had never married and had wanted to move to the coast after developing breathing problems, having fought off Spanish flu in 1918 during the hardships of the First World War. She was one of the first people to answer Pat's advertisement. Pat had taken pity on her as she seemed so frail. Keeping the rent to a minimum had turned out to be a great arrangement; Mademoiselle was quite an accomplished pianist and would play the old upright piano gently in the background as guests ate their evening meals in the dining room. Her repertoire was varied and included beautiful pieces from Chopin and Rachmaninov along with popular tunes of the time, such as "It's a Long Way to Tipperary", which was one of Pat's favourites.

They had decided to open officially every year in late May. They had continuous bookings from the end of June to early October, with many people making return bookings for the following year. Life was challenging, as Pat had never run a business before. It took some time to learn how to order the correct amount of food and manage the accounts.

Hélène was a great asset because she was so experienced, and they worked out a routine where they met every Monday morning to compose long to-do lists. Pat was absolutely disciplined at keeping the books, as this was a topic she vividly remembered hearing her father speak about many times at home in the pub in Killeshin. Acting on recommendations from their great friends the Goodrums, many guests came from as far away as England. They also attracted guests from as nearby as Deauville. Villa Durenne was becoming especially popular by word of mouth. Kitty was so happy—it was hard work but great fun compared to the life and future she would have had if she had stayed in Killeshin. She had become fluent in French and was not only conversing in the language constantly but also reading everything in French. *Frankenstein* was one of the most popular books at the time, and Kitty could not put it down. Mademoiselle Brodeur was a voracious reader and recommended different novels to her. Most evenings, they enjoyed long conversations about the twists and turns in whatever novel they were currently reading.

Pat was pleased with Kitty's progress. She wrote home to her sister Christine, who had married a local man, Jack Nelson, and moved to Dublin, where he joined the Dublin Mounted Police. Jack had returned a different man from Aldershot in England, where he had recuperated after being gassed at the Somme. He was over twenty years Christine's senior, but in those days, that was not unusual. To Pat, looking at the photograph of their wedding outside Kilkenny Cathedral, Jack appeared old. News of constant unrest in Dublin between the English authorities and the Irish freedom fighters was a source of great worry.

Pat had always enjoyed Jack Goodrum's company, and over the years they had become very close. They started writing to each other even more frequently, and their letters were starting to include not only friendly and amusing stories but little hints of romance. He was coming to stay in two weeks' time, and Pat had wondered if the friendship would ever develop into anything more. She was very fond of him, and she loved being in his company. They had such fun together, and boy, could he dance. Many times, alone in her bedroom, she had practised how she would greet him when they met. "Hi there—good to see you again," or "Ah, Jack, I have been looking forward to your visit for so long," or even "I have missed our time together." In the end, though, she said nothing as his boyish grin and eager arms swept her into a bear hug. It was as if they had closed one page of a book and opened another to an entirely different chapter. No explanation needed—they were inseparable. Kitty said it made her feel quite ill, all that lovey stuff, but Pat was in a constant state of happiness.

On the boat over, Jack had met a British officer named Jeff Smyth. They did not know each other but had mutual friends, which led Jack to recommend that Jeff stay at Villa Durenne before he travelled onwards to Paris. Jack was a total gentleman, but Jeff was another matter. Pat did not like Jeff from the moment she met him, describing him as "a rake". A very tall, agile man with his hair slicked over to the left and very well-tailored clothes, Jeff attracted a lot of attention from the ladies. Ladies young and old of every description—and, it had to be said, even Mademoiselle Brodeur—all but swooned at his every word. Jeff's tales from the four corners of the earth seemed to contain such knowledge and adventure that at times, even Pat could not help but be drawn in.

The couple of days Jeff was initially to spend with them turned into two weeks. Pat thought she would never get rid of him until fate, coupled with Jeff's scheming personality, brought an end to his stay. It was unfortunate that poor Kitty was involved in Jeff's downfall—she was still so innocent and saw nothing but good in everyone. What happened was short and very sweet, at least to Pat. She had noticed that Jeff was taking a little too much interest in Kitty and alerted Jack, Mademoiselle Brodeur, and Hélène to watch him. After dinner one evening, when Kitty was returning from her walk with Mademoiselle, Jeff asked her to play some cards with him. Expecting the worst, Pat waited within earshot, just outside the parlour door. Within ten minutes, she heard the screech of Kitty's chair as she jumped out of Jeff's amorous reach. Within the hour, Jeff was packed and off the premises with all his possessions, plus a shiner of a black eye.

Chapter 26

Kitty, One of Life's Blessed

For the next couple of weeks, Pat watched Kitty closely to see if her experience with Jeff had a lasting effect on her. One particular afternoon, as Kitty came running back up the path after having been in town with one of her many friends, it was obvious from the way she laughed and whistled that all was well. Kitty was the perfect person to have in the boarding house. She had a way with people of all ages. Just one look at her happy face, and anyone would know that here was one of life's blessed. Bright, quick-witted, and intelligent, with beauty inside and out, she made friends easily, eagerly looking forward to each day as if it was the start of an extraordinary adventure. Once she had settled into both her studies and work commitments, she had taken every opportunity that came her way and was a very much sought-after partner at the many dances around the local area. Her bedroom was the meeting place for her two special friends, and there they would try on each other's dresses and shoes, swapping jewellery and scarves to make every outfit look entirely different for each event. Nobody in the boarding house needed to be told when the ladies were getting ready, as everyone could hear the laughter and music, even in the garden. No matter what Kitty wore, she always had an air of elegance about her. During the summer months, she played tennis as often as possible. They had a grass court at Villa

Durenne, but she much preferred to go down to the local tennis club, as she had become great friends with a couple of the members. Never without a doubles partner, she took part in competitions, sometimes travelling to other towns to play in tournaments. Life was a whirlwind of fun for her. Some of the men she met asked her out on dates, but she never bothered taking on any type of serious boyfriend, as she did not want to miss any new opportunity that came her way. Mademoiselle Brodeur showed her how to sew and tailor, and she really enjoyed this, as it meant that she was able to create and adjust clothes whenever she wanted. The only skill that Kitty did not master was cooking. Hélène, the housekeeper, tried her best to show her how to make the simplest of dishes, but many scorched pots and pans were testament to failed attempts.

Pat was able to go away for a few days now and again, as the house could run very well without her. Late one summer, she took off to Bern with Jack Goodrum to visit the professor. They met in Paris and travelled on to Switzerland together. It was a happy trip, old friends to meet and places to revisit. Returning to the villa, she realised that she felt as if she was returning home. She was relieved that everything had gone so well while she was away. She wrote to her sister Christine in Co Laois that she was very proud of Kitty, who had really come into her own. Life was good for everyone.

Chapter 27

Romance in France but Famine in Ireland

Pat threw down a copy of the February 1925 edition of the *Manchester Guardian* on the scrubbed pine kitchen table and pounded the table with her fist, spittle spraying from her mouth. "Mon dieu! It's disgraceful. The people are starving, and nothing is being done for them."

A terrible newspaper picture stared back at Kitty and Hélène, showing four skeletal children and their mother suffering from starvation in a cabin in Gorumna Island, Galway. The article claimed that at least 750,000 people in Ireland faced starvation. Every family in Ireland could still tell shocking tales of the devastating famine of 1847. It was hard to believe such a thing could happen again. Pat was incensed. Coming from a rural background, she knew well what a disastrous potato crop could do to a community.

"Let's do something instead of just talking about it," she said and proceeded to form a plan. Her plan involved contacting the nuns in both Bern and Geneva to ask them to start a collection of clothes and money that she would send back to Ireland. Everyone in Villa Durenne became involved, and soon the outside sheds were full of parcels of clothes and bedding, which they would ship to Ireland. Convents in the neediest areas would distribute the items. "What a brilliant organiser you are, Pat. I don't know how you think of all the things you have to remember. We are so lucky to be able to help people back home!" said Kitty one day after they had shipped a mountain of donations. Pat felt privileged—all she had to worry about was how she should invest her savings. Life was so good for her and Kitty that they felt it immoral to have so much and to be so happy.

They had signed the lease on Villa Durenne at Monsieur Renard's office, and he had advised Pat to buy an apartment in Paris, as prices were due to rise rapidly due to the end of World War One. She had looked at a flat at 8 Villa Guizot, Rue de Acacias. Living in Paris at some stage instantly appealed to Pat. The flat was a good investment, and Monsieur Renard had it rented immediately. She had never intended to stay in Villa Durenne for the rest of her life.

These were very busy years, between running the villa, teaching, and her involvement in charity work. Jack Goodrum visited often and pleaded with Pat to marry him. There was a commitment between them, but it didn't last. As time went on, he became disillusioned, and the dissatisfaction sometimes showed in his expression. Pat rarely had enough time to devote to making any structured plans. After noticing Jack's frequent sad and hurt expressions, she knew she needed to make a decision about her future. She gave it a lot of thought until finally, one day when he was returning to the UK after a short break, she approached him and said, "Jack, I love you and will always be very fond of you, but I love my independence and life too much to change it. Let's remain just friends." She reassured him that there was not and never would be anyone else. Once again, she remembered the gypsy's prophecy. Jack was devastated, but deep down, he realised it was probably for the best. He knew it would be very difficult for him—or indeed, anyone else—to win Pat's affections. With a heavy heart, he returned home immediately. Still, he was far too optimistic a man to allow a setback to fully change his mind, and for years he remained a constant in Pat's world.

Pat wrote often to her sister Christine, updating her on how she and

Kitty were getting on. She had so much to tell and was nearly always in such a hurry that she often returned to her letter after it was finished to add information around the margins of the pages. By now, Kitty had started taking in students herself, such was her progress under Pat's skilled guidance. The two sisters sent money back to Ireland. Between the money from the Colgans and their boarding house income, they had few, if any money worries. A lot of mail was delivered to Villa Durenne, including bills, letters requesting accommodation, letters of thanks, and general correspondence between friends. It took a while before Pat began to notice Kitty's eagerness to bring in the mail each morning. One Sunday lunchtime, the doorbell rang, and Kitty and Pat arose at the same time to answer it. Kitty blushed, admitting, "It's for me," whereupon she hurried out to open the door. Standing there was a handsome young man with a bunch of roses in his hand. "Pat, come meet Andre Lagarde. He is my dear friend whom I met at the library in Deauville."

Pat shook the young man's outstretched hand and invited him to stay for lunch. She knew she would not need to ask him any questions, as Mademoiselle Brodeur was definitely going to interrogate him about everything that anyone could possibly want to know and more. Her devotion to Kitty would ensure this.

Between mouthfuls of roast lamb served with crispy roast potatoes and gravy, Andre passed every test with flying colours. He was a sandy-haired, slimly built man about five feet two inches tall with dark green eyes; he and Kitty made a very attractive couple. She hung on his every word and looked wide-eyed from Pat to Mademoiselle Brodeur, as if Andre were relating the secrets of the universe. At one stage, Pat thought she would burst out laughing. She noticed that Mademoiselle was simply melting away with the romance of it all. No point in fighting it—the young couple were smitten. Andre was originally from Perpignan, and he spoke about his family with great affection. Both Pat and Kitty wrote letters in Villa Durenne that night and posted them Ireland the next day. Luckily, both letters were in total agreement that, yes, indeed, little Kitty was in love and that she had found a very suitable Mr Right.

Chapter 28

A Proposal

It was a secret that Pat found really difficult to keep. It was evident from Kitty's face as she sang to herself while doing her work in Villa Durenne that she was blissfully happy. Kitty had such a generous personality that she had to share her happiness with everyone she met. One warm summer afternoon, as Pat sat alone doing her accounts, Kitty came into see her and plonked herself down in front of the overladen desk. Kitty kept babbling away about this and that, including Andre's name every couple of seconds. Pat tried very hard not to become agitated, as she had to submit figures in a couple of days. Being meticulous about her bookkeeping, she hated being interrupted. Gently, she hinted to Kitty that they could speak later, after dinner, but Kitty just kept going until an exasperated Pat finally barked, "Okay, Kitty! I'm delighted you are so happy, but I really need to finish this."

Kitty jumped up from the chair and reached inside her blouse, pulling out a long golden chain upon which hung an engagement ring. Pat was speechless. Putting her finger to her lips to keep her older sister from squealing with delight, Kitty got up and closed the door while Pat threw her arms around her. Taking the sweet little gold ring with entwined double diamonds, she slipped it on her own second finger to make a wish. Turning the ring towards her heart, she whispered, "Kitty, when did you get this?" Kitty smiled and said that Andre had taken her into town the previous evening. He had booked their favourite restaurant. They were seated at their usual table near the window overlooking the park, which was filled with people relaxing and enjoying the late evening sun. They ordered their food, and he asked for a glass of champagne before their meal. Presenting her with a single long-stemmed red rose with a little parcel attached to it, he waited while she slowly unwrapped her gift. Speechless for once, she just stared at the sweet little ring as Andre knelt down and asked her to marry him. Taking his adoring face in her two hands, she whispered yes with tears running down her face.

Andre and Kitty spoke all evening about what they would do and when they would get married. They both decided that they would write to their families, and once they knew about it, only then tell everyone else. Kitty made one exception; she would tell Pat immediately, as she would help them with their plans. Kitty was so relieved to be able to tell someone that she nearly burst with excitement before she finally got Pat alone in the office that afternoon. Books forgotten, Pat and Kitty sat together for what seemed like hours, discussing how they would celebrate the engagement and the wedding. They decided to go for a walk around the softly glowing evening sunlit garden. Their arms linked, their heads bent in deep discussion, their happy faces glowed in the rosy light.

Meeting Andre's family was an event that Pat decided to arrange before the winter set in. She and Kitty took the train to Perpignan one Saturday morning early in September. A glorious day broke; the dew that lay on the fields seemed to create a haze as the sun's beams started to warm up. Arm in arm, they walked towards the train station with a carefully prepared gift that Hélène had made and wrapped in numerous layers of greaseproof paper to protect it during the long journey ahead. It was to be a surprise even for Kitty: A most magnificent three-tiered Victoria sponge, sandwiched with homemade raspberry jam and lashings of thick cream. Hélène had dusted the top of the cake in icing sugar and made tiny little fondant rose petals and hearts to scatter across it when they finally served it. Pat could think of only one word as she imagined

Kitty's face when she saw it: *heaven*.

They were lucky, as the train did not seem over full. Many people were heading to seaside towns such as Villiers-sur-Mer on such a beautiful day. They felt no apprehension about meeting Andre's relatives, as Pat was sure that only a caring, well-educated family could have produced such a decent human being. As they travelled through the French countryside, they couldn't help but notice what a vast country France was compared to Ireland. They arrived around one p.m., and an eager Andre and his very welcoming mother and father greeted them. Andre tucked his arm into Kitty's, and they chatted and laughed with his parents and Pat as they walked through the city, with its mix of Catalonian and French influences. Andre's home was a two-storey house with a one-storey annex at the side. A lovely garden surrounded the house, with a mix of well-tended rose trees and a very impressive vegetable patch. Andre's father insisted that they sit in the garden until lunch was ready. Pat carried the cake box and parcels into the kitchen, and as soon as the scent of the venison stew hit her nostrils, she realised that she was starving. It was a homely kitchen, with a dresser filled with all types of plates and dishes—signs of a comfortable family life evident from all the photographs on the walls.

Pat sat with Andre and Kitty in the garden drinking a boule of cider, which Andre's father had proudly declared was of his own making. Crisp and sharp, it added to the relaxing effect of the warm afternoon sun and the happiness of the couple laughing beside her. Before long, Andre's mother called them in to sit at the oval oak dining table, which she had set with what was obviously their good dinner service. She laid the last serving dishes on the table, and Andre's father rose and made a blessing for all gathered. As the evening shadows lengthened and the room cooled down ever so slightly, they suddenly realised that they had spent a long time chatting over lunch, and the time had come to unveil Hélène's special surprise. The sight of the beautiful cake, made with such love, in the centre of table with the china plates and linen napkins arranged beside it made everyone silent. Seizing the moment, Andre stood up, raised his glass, and said, "To my darling Kitty! Thank you for agreeing to be my wife. I look forward to our life together and will make you happy, I promise." His parents clapped their hands in delight. Kitty jumped up and threw her arms around him, and their deeply affectionate kiss just reinforced Pat's contentment with the new life her sister was embarking upon.

All too quickly, it was time to walk down to get the last train home. They all agreed that it had been a fantastic day, and Pat invited Andre to bring his parents down to Villa Durenne in October, when they would make definite plans for the wedding, which was to take place at the villa the following summer. Pat was pleased that Andre's family were happy with the decision to hold the wedding there. The time came to say goodbye, and the exhausted but happy families hugged one another. Kitty waved goodbye to Andre until his figure was just a small dot on the platform. She sat down beside Pat and snuggled into her; the two of them fell asleep and had to be awakened by a kind conductor in Paris. There they changed to the train that would take them to Normandy.

Chapter 29

Destination Paris

Monsieur Renard hopped from one foot to the other as he anxiously waited for the front door to Villa Durenne to open. The moment she heard the bell, Pat skipped down the stairs still wearing her tennis whites, rubbing the perspiration from her face with a towel. Flinging open the door with a beaming smile, she could not have been more surprised to see her notary standing there. "Ah, ah, Monsieur Renard, how lovely to see you! What brings you to Villa Durenne? Kitty, Kitty look who is here. Come in, Monsieur Renard, come in."

As she beckoned him to follow her, something about his furtive expression made her stomach clench. Kitty came out from the kitchen, and Pat was glad that this at least gave her time to gather her thoughts.

"Ah Monsieur Renard," Kitty said, "have you met my fiancé, Andre?" Kitty made tea and she, Pat, Andre, and Monsieur Renard chatted awkwardly at the table. It became obvious that this was not an ordinary social visit. Hands shaking with nerves, Monsieur raised his teacup to his prominent lips, which were beaded with sweat.

Finally, Pat snapped, "Good God, Monsieur Renard, please tell me you have not come here to have a heart attack."

To everyone's amazement, he burst into tears. "Mademoiselle Fitzpatrick, I am so sorry, so very sorry, but I am in terrible trouble. It is the crash—I have lost everything." Leaning onto the table, he sobbed and dropped the teacup, which shattered on the tiled kitchen floor.

The only person at the table who did not appear confused was Pat. She recalled the scene in Renard's office when she was signing the paperwork on her Paris flat. His words replayed in her mind: "Leave it to me, Mademoiselle Fitzpatrick. I will take care of your inheritance and invest it wisely. I have a contact in America. A clever man, Mr. Montgomery, who deals in stocks and shares. Not only will your money be safe, but it will make money."

Pat closed her eyes as the vision of smug Monsieur Renard rose up before her. In a tone that would freeze ice on the Alps, she spoke slowly and very precisely. "The crash, Monsieur Renard, I have read all about it. I am fully aware of what this means for myself and my family. You have ruined us."

Turning her back on the shocked faces of Kitty and Andre, Pat dug her nails into the palms of her hands and tried to maintain control. Time seemed suspended until she heard the scrape of the chair on the hard tiles. Afraid of her reaction should she look back at Renard too quickly, she waited until she heard Andre's voice rise above Kitty's gentle sobs, "You bastard! You come here to cry, to ask forgiveness?"

At that point, Pat decided to intervene in case the situation became physical. She turned slowly to stare directly into Monsieur Renard's reddened eyes. The overweight man fell to his knees, pleading for absolution with hands clasped in prayer as a mixture of snot and tears ran down his face. All Pat wanted to do was to get this despicable vision of weak humanity out of her sight as soon as possible.

It took over an hour to get Monsieur Renard to settle down and stop shaking long enough to allow him to write a coherent and detailed account of how he had invested Pat's money. The buff envelope that held all the accounts lay torn open on the table in front of him. He had brought the documents with him expecting to just leave them with Pat and return to Paris as quickly as possible, but he had underestimated her. There was no way he was going home without being made to provide detailed information, account for the amounts he had invested, and answer some serious questions. Pat appeared calm and focused, but inside, she felt as though she were in a dreamlike state. Her stomach was churning. Every so often, tiny shots of bile rose in the back of her throat.

Kitty sat motionless at the table, looking so pale that Andre kept rubbing her back gently and squeezing her shoulders, whispering that he would protect her. He threw murderous looks in Monsieur Renard's direction. Only when dusk had made it too difficult to continue did they all stop. Gathering the paperwork into one large pile, they discussed what they needed to do next. Pat excused herself, as for the moment she was determined to put the villa's guests first.

At dinner time, she bustled around the dining room, serving food and chatting away as normal. She had left Kitty with Andre and Monsieur Renard. Renard continued to scribble down various figures and notes. Needing to be alone, Pat placed some baked potatoes on a plate and quietly made her way to the empty back parlour. There, she sat at a table and forced herself to eat, remembering her mother's words that potatoes could "cure everything". No matter how Monsieur Renard presented the information, the money could not be retrieved. As Pat sat there eating in silence, she thought about everything clearly. Villa Durenne had only two years left on the paid lease. Thank God she had bought the flat in Paris, and she still had a small amount of savings, but she had to plan quickly to make sure she did not lose any more money. The decision was not difficult. To make some money, she had to sell Villa Durenne's lease as soon as possible. They would have to move the wedding date forward to coincide with the final signing of the papers. Then Pat would move to Paris to seek work and make a new life for herself, and Andre and Kitty would move in with his parents. Pat made these decisions quickly, and heart-wrenching upset went with them.

Monsieur Renard worked with Pat through the night. In the morning, he headed for the early train to Paris, vowing to help her complete the sale of the lease for Villa Durenne with as little trouble as possible. Pat did not believe him, nor was she interested in his hollow pleading. Nevertheless, she saw Monsieur Renard onto the train and even faked a tight smile. Afterwards, she hurried to make an appointment with an estate agent who had approached her about Villa Durenne the previous year. She could not believe that she was going to actually have to sell her lease. The business was so well established that it was due to make yet another increase in profits. The auctioneer was delighted to see Pat and made arrangements for prospective clients to view the villa and examine the books on the following Saturday.

The toughest job lay ahead. Pat dragged her feet along the path and went slowly through the gate, looking up at the beautiful house she loved. Squaring her shoulders, she opened the hall door and called for Hélène, Marc, and Mademoiselle Brodeur to come into the office. She told them that the villa was to be sold. Ignoring the shocked look on their faces, she told them that the new owners had offered them places, and on top of this, pay rises to stay on. Her heart pounding and stomach queasy with the tension of the previous twenty-four hours, she walked swiftly out the back door, grabbing the dog's lead as she went, before shutting the door behind her with a firm bang.

Pat knew it would take some time before all the paperwork for Villa Durenne was completed but wasted no time preparing the flat in Paris. Monsieur Renard had transferred all her details to a notary colleague who served notice on the flat's tenants immediately. Once the flat was unoccupied, she took the first available train to Paris.

The first thing she did when she arrived at the flat was to throw open all the windows. She quickly changed into shorts and an old blouse, tied her hair back, and she was ready. In true Pat fashion, she immediately dedicated herself to cleaning and scrubbing until she had polished every surface, eradicating any smell that reminded her of the previous occupants. She applied lavender polish on every piece of wood from the floor to the architraves. Jamming the front door to the hallway open, along with the open windows, created a wonderful flow of fresh air as she worked. It didn't bother her one bit that the flat was freezing. Pat enjoyed every moment of this work, as she wanted the flat to feel brand new. Many hours later, she stood back to admire her work and couldn't resist bursting into song. Then, finally giving in to exhaustion, she slid to the floor, her back against the wall. She reached for her lighter and cigarettes. "Merde," she muttered, noticing that her usually bright red, perfectly manicured fingernails had now become filthy black stubs. Pulling tightly on her Gitane, letting out a slow puff of smoke, and looking around her, she decided it was worth it. There was not a speck of dirt anywhere.

The following morning at precisely nine a.m., the van arrived with some of their furniture from Villa Durenne. As the removal men huffed and puffed their way up the many flights of stairs, Pat drove them crazy with her very exact instructions, "Non, non, idiot, not there, careful!" She couldn't wait to get rid of the movers so that she could arrange the place exactly as she wanted. Many hours later, she was satisfied enough to put on her coat and go to the nearby flower shop to treat herself to a bunch of the most magnificent, deep pink gladioli. Before she left for the shops, she temporarily hung her framed pictures. She spent that evening with a glass of red wine, swapping pictures back and forth until she decided upon the appropriate places. Only then did she reach for a hammer and nails. Satisfied that the flat was ready for her to return after Kitty and Andre's wedding, she returned to Villa Durenne to continue preparations.

Chapter 30

The Wedding

What a relief to celebrate Kitty and Andre's wedding after all the turmoil of the past couple of months, thought Pat. She had just returned to Paris early that afternoon, and before settling down with a glass of well-earned wine, she wanted to put away her beautiful wedding outfit. As she wrapped her pale blue suit in tissue paper and added her white, pure silk blouse with pale blue polka dots to the long cardboard box, she stopped for a moment. Flopping down on the bed, she took the photo of herself, Kitty, and Andre on that magical day from her bedside table and just stared at the beautiful couple, drinking in the warm glow she felt every time she looked at it. Andre had one arm around Kitty and one around Pat. *Nobody could ask for more*, she thought.

The ceremony had taken place just before the sale of Villa Durenne. The villa had never looked as good as it did on that magical, sunny morning. Pat was first up as usual and could not resist grabbing her black togs and stripey blue towel and cycling down to the beach for a quick swim. The azure blue sea seemed to twinkle with a billion diamonds, as if to reflect that the universe itself was in tune with the coming nuptials. Lying on her back in the warm water, Pat was able to feel grateful that at least they could hold the wedding at Villa Durenne. As she cycled up the slight hill toward the villa, its open windows with lace curtains billowing in the tepid, salty air, Pat felt proud of this beautiful home that she had created and found the strength to accept she had to let it go. At first, Kitty and Andre thought to marry in his hometown near Perpignan, but Pat really wanted to host the celebration. After all the upset about having to sell the property, she insisted that the wedding would take place in Villa Durenne. It was not possible to have it in Ireland; at least she could make it as Irish a celebration as possible for Kitty.

They all agreed that it was the perfect place for Kitty and Andre's wedding breakfast. The suppliers were only too delighted to help the much-loved Kitty with her wedding celebrations. The entire setup of the guest house was suitable to entertain the wedding guests, and the ten-minute walk to the local church combined with the romantic garden ensured that it would be a beautiful day. On the morning of the wedding, when Kitty was ready, she called Pat from the top of the stairs and descended slowly, looking at her with such happiness that Pat just had to shed a tear. The two bridesmaids walked slightly ahead to the church while Kitty and Pat took a few last moments in the house to give each other a tight hug. Pat then handed Kitty her little bouquet of forget-me-nots and roses tied together with cream ribbon, and they left Villa Durenne to the sound of the church bell ringing.

It was a heart-tugging sight that met Andre and the wedding party as Jack Goodrum took Kitty's arm at the church and led her up the aisle. She looked so beautiful in her cream suit and wide-brimmed hat and cream shoes, her kid gloves stitched with little pearl buttons. The wedding breakfast was in the courtyard, with the trestle tables covered in white Irish linen cloths, a wedding gift from the Swiss nuns, and they had embroidered them with Andre and Kitty's initials entwined by swallows. Baskets of late-flowering roses and forget-me-nots adorned the centre of the tables. The four tables were set in a square with the bride and groom's table at the top, near the kitchen door. All the food had an Irish touch—home-made soda bread along with large pieces of bacon, tomato, and sausages and steaming hot potato cakes washed down with coffee or tea. The wedding cake appeared at last. A two-tier fruit cake that Pat had lovingly made and iced, with Andre and Kitty's name piped on the top.

Aunt Pat's War

A glass of sparkling wine, and the speeches began. Jack spoke first about how lucky Andre was and how Kitty's Irish family were looking forward to meeting him as soon as possible. Then Andre spoke emotionally about his love for Kitty and his great plans for their future. Lastly, he thanked all the people who had helped make this such a special day for them. Everyone stood and raised their glass to the beautiful couple, and then it was time for them to leave for their brief honeymoon in the neighbouring town. The photographer insisted on taking some photos in the beautiful rose-filled garden, and they climbed into the borrowed Citroën with tin cans tied to the back bumper; the happy couple's hair was full of colourful confetti the guests threw at them as they waved goodbye. There were enough bedrooms for Andre's family to stay over at the villa, and the music from the old piano in the dining room came in handy as the merry revellers took to the floor. Jack and Pat clinked glasses and agreed it was a fantastic way to say goodbye to the happy house.

Chapter 31

Free and in Love

Opening the crinkly brown salary envelope with its clear plastic window, through which her name and employee number were visible, Pat reflected on how things had changed in the last couple of years. She had to admit it, life had worked out well after Villa Durenne, and now she really felt settled again, something she never would have thought possible. It had taken six months to complete all the paperwork, settle the accounts, and move to Paris. She had been surprised to find they had a little money left over, and they had used it to spend some holiday time in Ireland. After the shock of Monsieur Renard's stupidity, a visit home was just what she and Kitty needed. Renard had tried to help them by organising a job for Pat in Banc de Paris, but once the legal business was finished, they never heard from him again until a Saturday in 1931, when Pat read the announcement of his death in the paper. They greeted this news with a lack of emotion. They had long since decided that they needed to put the past behind them and to focus on themselves and their future.

Pat left Villiers-sur-Mer after signing the papers that transferred Villa Durenne to its new owners; she thought it would be a terrible wrench, but she did not find it difficult at all. She realised that she had developed the ability to adapt well to change. As the train pulled into Paris-Gare-de-Lyon on her return from a trip to Perpignan, she could almost smell the excitement of the capital city as it greeted her. She straightened her plaid skirt and prepared to step down from the train, feeling as though she could take on the world. Walking along the platform, she took great joy in the way her deep maroon skirt hugged her figure. She wore a peplum jacket and a felt hat trimmed with feathers. Pat looked good and she knew it. The swish of the skirt's silk lining made a soft sound as it moved over her silk stockings. Just for a moment, she allowed herself to admire her slim legs in her new, black suede court shoes. Gathering her luggage from the porter, she quickly strode forward, handbag over her arm, ready to embark on her new adventure as a fully independent single woman.

As Kitty now lived with Andre's family, Pat finally found time to take a lover. The affair had started innocently, more as a joke than anything else. Marian Jaeger, her best friend from boarding school days, had arrived to spend a few days with Pat. It was 1936. Pat would turn forty the following year. As they sat in the flat one evening drinking wine, chatting about lost love and growing older, Marian told Pat about a good friend in Paris who had a brother called Richard. He had just split from his long-time girlfriend in Ireland and was now working in Paris. Marian had met him through the Goodrums, which she knew would impress Pat. Now she challenged Pat to go on a blind date.

Not being one to step away from a challenge, Pat could not resist accepting the dare. The quantity of wine she'd consumed also contributed to her decision.

Marian had arranged to meet Richard the following morning in the market near the Tomb of the Unknown Soldier. Pat's flat was nearby, and despite her pounding head and fuzzy tongue, she agreed to keep her promise. Putting on a navy and cream silk, full-skirted dress with a neat linen jacket, Pat skimmed her lips with red lipstick and adjusted her cream beret; she blew a kiss at herself in the hall mirror. Then, linking arms, the two women jauntily descended the stairs and out to the street, laughing loudly as they headed towards the market.

Once Pat set her eyes on Richard, she instantly remembered him. She had met him once in her sister Christine's home when she was home for the Christmas holidays . He had struck her then, as he did now, with his undeniable resemblance to the actor Jimmy Stewart. Tall and lean, with slicked back light brown hair, his expression was one of permanent amusement, helped enormously by his twinkling blue eyes. Pat was immediately taken with him. It also helped that she had just seen Jimmy Stewart and Margaret Sullivan's very popular romantic film, *Next Time We Love*.

Over the following week, the two became very attached. Pat had had a few boyfriends in the past, but apart from the youthful disaster in Switzerland, she had resisted immersing herself too much in any relationship, as she found most men much preferable as friends. It was also true that her strong, independent personality frightened most men away. Having gone off to boarding school at such a young age and being able to return home only for summer holidays, Pat was used to not being hugged or touched by people. Intimacy—even friendship—was often difficult for her. She felt she needed to keep up an independent, untouchable veneer to remain strong, but her relationship with Dick changed this. The two of them spent their days walking for miles around the never-ending sights of Paris, returning to Pat's apartment late in the evenings, exhausted. He would take her hand and undress her slowly, cupping her face in his hands before kissing her deeply. They spent many nights making passionate love, sleeping wrapped in each other's arms. This was a magic time for Pat. She felt that she had become whole. Now she could face anything. Sadly, it was not to last. She had not seen Marian Jaeger since she had introduced her to Dick that day at the market, but now the three of them stood in Pat's living room, shouting at each other.

"You bastard, Dick! You have lied and used Pat. How could you sleep with her when you are engaged at home?" screamed Marian.

"I love her and want to be with her—I did not use her." Dick spoke slowly, his face red with emotion.

Pat did not know what to make of it. "Is this true? Are you engaged to someone in Ireland?"

Marian answered for him, "He is. To that Sweeney girl with the big farm, you know them."

Dick couldn't meet Pat's eyes, and she walked silently to her bedroom. Gathering all his clothes and toiletries, she threw them into his small bag. She carried his bag into the living room and handed it to him. "Go," she said. He was fully aware that he had made a huge mistake.

Closing the door, Pat convulsed with tears. After a while, she allowed Marian to lead her to the armchair, which she refused to leave for twenty-four hours. This affair damaged her irrevocably. She never again allowed herself to indulge in any type of serious relationship that might cause her so much pain.

Chapter 32

Paris 1940

The first thing Pat did once she had recovered from her broken heart was make a dramatic change. She dyed her hair bright red and had it cut into a sharp, boyish style. The first time Marian saw it. she had to bite her lip not to comment.

Marian became a constant in Pat's life after this; they shared similar interests and liked nothing more than to spend every other weekend with Kitty and Andre. They all enjoyed each other's company. They had started cycling to local rivers, where Andre was teaching them how to fish. The meals they made from these prized catches were all the tastier when served with the embellished tales of how each fish was caught. Sometimes, Kitty and Andre came to Paris, and the four attended local jazz clubs. Together they had gathered a few interesting and fun-loving friends. Life would have been perfect—except for the constant rumblings of war.

The day everyone had been dreading finally arrived on 14 June 1940. Pat and Sister Bernarde stood silently on the Champs Elysees as Hitler and his troops marched triumphantly through Paris. It was a strange experience to watch that small, moustached man waving to the people of the city as if he were their king. The sound of jackboots reverberated through the streets, and it made Pat even more determined to do something to help put a stop to this terrible situation. Sister Bernarde promised she would tell her when she heard of a trustworthy group of people who were planning to resist the Germans in any way. She could not have spoken more vehemently as she warned Pat not to mention this to anyone, as strange things were happening everywhere. Even the French were reporting each other for any type of unusual behaviour.

Pat and Marian had been down to see Kitty and Andre one weekend in early September 1940. The four of them went for a long walk in the countryside. It was a beautiful day, blue sky and sunshine. The birds were singing and chasing each other, trying to catch the midges that skimmed the surface of the river. Kitty had skipped along the path leading back to Andre's home; she had never looked so happy. They were in love and spent their time making plans, especially about getting their own place eventually. Andre's parents were kind to Kitty and entertained Pat and Marian that day as if they were family.

Over dinner, they discussed in great detail the Nazis' rise to power and the tensions between the communists and other groups. Andre and his family were de Gaulle supporters. The Resistance had started that summer, and the mention of the word caused a sense of fear, even at that family meal. Little did they know that Pat was leaving early to join a Resistance group in Paris. It was strange not to speak to Kitty about it, but she knew she could not risk it.

Sister Bernarde had told Pat about a place called Café Jacques in Paris. Nobody spoke openly about the Resistance, but she had heard that this was the best place to make contact. Those in the Resistance movement trusted nobody. Each person had an item that became known as their identity badge. Pat's was the green lighter with the dragon emblem. Once she attended regularly, she was determined to become one of the most reliable members. One thing baffled them all: some Parisians' acceptance of and support for Hitler and the Nazis.

Things began to change on New Year's Eve 1940. Pat was sitting in her best friend's flat with two other close friends listening to BBC's Radio

Londres when de Gaulle called for all French people to stay indoors on New Year's Eve between three and four p.m. in an act of passive resistance. Upon hearing this first call to action, Pat and her friends jumped to their feet, hugging each other. At last, the Resistance was beginning! They were ready to make a difference. That night, not even the bitter cold wind could deflate Pat's elation as she sneaked home through the sinister streets.

Chapter 33

A Brief Marriage

The only relic of the beautiful, vivacious Kitty Lagarde was a pair of elegant wedding shoes. They peeped out from beneath a black widow's outfit, which hung from her thin shoulders as though it belonged to another woman. Andre's and Kitty's wedding photograph sat on top of the coffin, the lid closed out of necessity to conceal Andre's tortured body.

Pat sat through the service holding Kitty's limp hand tightly, internally repeating the mantra, *I must be strong, I must stay strong.* She had loved Kitty all her life and had delighted in the happiness and the bright future she had seen for this young, loving couple. Andre's loss was a terrible blow not just to Kitty but to the Lagarde and Fitzpatrick families. Pat focused on the many lit candles at the shrine to St Anthony to the left of Andre's casket. However, the scent of lilies soon dragged her mind back to the reality of where she was.

Every now and then, she sensed Kitty glancing at the wedding photograph intensely, as if her sheer longing was enough to bring Andre back. Pat smelt a stale, sickly scent from her sister's breath. From the moment the young woman had found Andre's mutilated body, she had vomited intermittently, such was her devastation. Pat was unsure Kitty could ever recover from such a shock.

Trying not to break down and give in to tears, Pat stared at her sister's wedding photograph. She noted the kindness in Andre's eyes, his arm protectively around Kitty's waist as she peeped out from underneath her wide-brimmed hat. They made a handsome couple. Up until now they had been living with Andre's family, planning to remain there until they could save enough money to get their own place.

At the time, France was in turmoil. There were murders aplenty. Communist gangs swooped on innocent people as they went about their daily lives. Andre was an active member of the Free French, and Kitty had noticed that he was more security-conscious than he had ever been. De Gaulle's Free French were seen to be at odds with the communists, and as the war progressed, both began to fear the other taking power. The lovely young couple's idyllic married life ended six months after their wedding day. One evening, Kitty had been waiting for Andre to come home from work. She had finished teaching early that day and dashed back to cook his favourite dinner, just as she had promised him when they kissed goodbye that morning. Listening to the radio while ironing, she was not particularly worried that he was an hour late. Sometimes he would call into his parents' part of the house on his way home. She imagined that this was the case.

However, as the hours went by with no sign of Andre, she realised something was wrong. When dusk rolled in, she began to feel very apprehensive. He was never that late. The dinner would be ruined. Her heart started to race as she put away the iron. Throwing on her woollen coat, she grabbed a torch and slipped it into her pocket. Closing the front door gently, she peered into the lit kitchen of Andre's parents' annex as she passed. To her shock, she saw them sitting by the stove half-asleep, obviously having eaten their meal, empty plates on the table waiting to be washed. Kitty didn't know where to look or whom to ask, so she just followed her instinct and headed towards the village square. She guessed she might hear something there. Nothing could have prepared her for what happened next. As she approached the centre of the village, someone grabbed her from behind. She stared at the person holding her arm, who then spat into her face. Distraught, she recognised one of the leaders of the local communist group who had been putting up posters during the week.

"Ah, Madame Legardre, you will not find your pretty husband here or that stupid mayor." The communist leader spun her around and pushed her towards a disused yard. Kitty heard him laughing as she started to run, sobbing loudly now. She shouted for help. It was almost dark, and the only light came from the beam of her torch as she searched around the yard. Horses were kept there, and she could smell the dung as she swirled the light into every corner. Nothing. Then she saw it—a bare foot spattered in blood protruding from the dung heap. She thought she was running towards it, but time seemed to slow down so much that she felt as though she might choke on her own breath. Lying face upwards was her beloved Andre. Beside him, the body of the mayor, both deadly still. She tried to scream, but no sound came out. His corpse lay there, mouth wide open, eyes bulging. She took off her coat and tried to wrap it around his badly beaten and bruised body. In the distance, she heard voices. The voices mixed with her own sounds of distress.

As she lay cradling his lifeless body, Andre's left hand flopped out from the coat. The hand was covered in blood; his fourth finger had been cut off, leaving jagged flesh and congealed blood. His shiny new wedding ring was missing.

Days went by in a haze. Kitty was only vaguely aware of Pat's arrival from Paris, summoned by Andre's traumatised family. Pat was at a loss to know how she could help Kitty to heal. All she could do was to love and nurture her as best she could. She did know that no matter what happened, she would never forgive such a base, vile act. The experience changed Pat forever.

Weeks ran into months. By the time Christmas 1941 arrived, Pat and the Legardre family were so frightened for Kitty's mental state that they took the awful but necessary decision to put her in a sanatorium to allow her to get the help she needed. Pat kissed her sister goodbye with tears running down her cheeks. She felt she had no choice except to trust the medical staff.

Then she left quickly to catch a train to Paris. The family in Killeshin were worried about Kitty, but they trusted Pat to keep an eye on her. That year, Pat did not go to Ireland for Christmas. Instead, she divided her time between her many friends in Paris and visits to Kitty in the sanitorium.

Chapter 34

Paris Is Liberated, 25 August 1944

Liberation Day finally arrived on a hot, sultry August day. The battles to free Paris were not fully over, but the pure sense of freedom was tangible all around the tired but elated city. Pat sat by the open window in her flat in the early hours of 25 August 1944, smoking her final cigarette of a very long day. She felt hope and an energy for the future that she had not allowed herself to think about in ages. As she walked to her local church to give thanks, she was amazed at how she noticed everything. Flowers had never smelt as sweet or looked more vividly beautiful. She would never forget de Gaulle's rousing speech from Hotel de Ville. "Why do you wish to hide the emotion which seizes us all, men and women, who are here, at home, in Paris that stood up to liberate itself and that succeeded in doing this with its own hands?" His words had an instant effect—Paris appeared to glisten with pride. French soldiers in dress regalia, their black, plumed helmets shining in the hazy sunshine as the military band played a victorious tune, led the way for General de Gaulle and the rest of the dignitaries. The sights and sounds filled her heart with pride. They had done it, and yes, it had been worth it. Even the collaborators and German snipers who shot and wounded so many from their hiding spots in the buildings surrounding the celebration marches could not dilute the elation of Parisians.

The morning after Liberation Day, Pat sat down to plan how she was going to start again. It was so different this time, as she had Kitty to consider as well. She decided that she would bring Kitty back to Paris as soon as possible and ask Sister Bernarde for her advice. No time to waste, Pat tidied herself up and made her way to the convent. Luckily, Sister Bernarde had been thinking about Kitty; she had a lovely family in Paris who wanted help with the children's schooling. Pat agreed to take it on and to gradually introduce Kitty to the children with the hope that she would eventually take over the position.

It took a number of weeks before Kitty came to live in Paris. It was sad to see her so low, but between Pat and all her many wonderful friends, Kitty began to make a huge effort to take part in the simplest of tasks. Sister Bernarde took Kitty with her whenever she went to see the family Pat was working with, and Kitty finally agreed in April 1945 to teach them alongside Pat.

The much-anticipated VE Day arrived on 8 May 1945. Pat and Kitty stood side by side with Sister Bernarde. Kitty was going to spend the night with the family she taught, but before she went there, she wanted to watch the VE parade. Parisians were relieved and overjoyed at the sight of confident, swanky Americans sweeping through the streets with their vast array of armaments swathed in the Stars and Stripes. Such a contrast to the sight of the blue-grey hue of suppression when the Nazis marched into Paris in June 1940. The French were effervescent with delight—their beloved Paris was liberated! Horns blew, whistles shrilled, lovers loved.

Pat was relieved that Kitty was not home as she crawled up the steps to her flat early the following morning, the laces of her flat, white summer shoes tied together and slung over her shoulders to avoid losing them. She looked out the side window of the stairwell at the city, still alive with revellers. It had taken her so long to get up the stairs. She kept stopping on the way to either hiccup or giggle. The entire city had gone crazy, and Pat had been swept along by its infectious excitement. The sun was rising, casting a golden splendour over a Paris that neither slept nor wanted to.

Once in her small bedroom, she placed her shoes on the bedside table, laces untied and arranged with perfect precision in the centre of each shoe—as only the very tipsy or tired can do. She lay fully clothed on her bed, hugging herself every few minutes, pinching her arms to make sure she was actually awake and not just dreaming. She felt as if a tight, choking feeling had dissipated, replaced by a sensation of well-being and hope for the future.

Afterwards, life was so busy that nobody had time to think about anything but trying to get things back to normal as quickly as possible. Pat felt happy. In the city, there was such satisfaction in helping others to find work. One morning in June 1946, a letter arrived from the Foreign Office in London. It informed her that Miss Winifred Fitzpatrick had been recommended by the British Secretary of State for Foreign Affairs for appointment as a Member of the British Empire on His Majesty's Birthday in recognition of her valuable services during the war.

Pat had to sit down to read and re-read the letter. She was to be awarded an MBE, an award given to members of the British empire, for her work with the Resistance. Pat had no sense of her own worth, and she found it very difficult to take in that she was to receive such recognition. Deciding she needed to talk to somebody about it, she quickly put on her light blue jacket and headed to see Jacque at the café where they had coordinated most of her efforts for the Resistance. Why did her feet feel lighter as she walked along, and why did everything around her seem especially pleasing?

She hurried to the café and waited impatiently for Jacque to finish serving coffee to two little old ladies who always sat in that exact seat at the same time each day. She was tapping her fingers on the table when he sat down. "Ah, Mademoiselle Fitz. Why the impatience? Surely today is far too beautiful to waste."

It took every ounce of Pat's patience not to scream at him. Instead, she threw down the letter on the table. Then, folding her arms, she glared at him while he read. Jumping up, Jacque enveloped Pat in his arms, twirling her around the café floor. To the tune of the "Le Chant des Partisans," he sang at the top of his voice, "Mademoiselle Fitzpatrick is going to tea with the King of England!"

The café erupted. Pat was well-liked in Paris, her eccentricities accepted with great affection. The sight of her red, tightly cropped hair bopping along as Jacques sang and danced her around the café created much happiness for everyone present. Most people were aware of the sacrifices she had made and the many dangerous chances she undertook. Just as Paris had joined together to fight the Nazis, the customers at Jacque's Café were more than happy to celebrate Pat's much deserved honour.

For many hours, the wine flowed and the music played. Pat was swept up in the celebrations as if she were celebrating on behalf of the entire city of Paris. Such was her joy that it was not until the following day she began to think about how her family in Ireland would react.

Chapter 35

Those Who Were Lost

The first thing to hit her was the smell of rotting, wounded flesh. No matter how she tried to blot it out, she couldn't. Screeching, shrieking, then almost subdued sobbing. Followed by silence—total, menacing, and sheer silence. Metallic grey mist covered everything, making it virtually impossible to make out clear shapes from all human mounds lying immobile. Pat froze in terror every time a burst of fierce, orange-red flames shot out from the smouldering buildings. The flames illuminated figures with skeletal features and cold, empty gazes, mouths left open forever in eternal pleading, hopelessly trying to get someone to help them escape their last terrified moments. Helpless, trapped in this nightmare, Pat would tear at the bedclothes with her hands, imagining them scraping through mangled bodies searching for all the people she had known who had been murdered in this terrible war. Eyes wide open as if she had never slept, she sat bolt upright and screamed. Jumping up out of her bed, she dropped to the cold bedroom floor, covered in sweat with her heart beating wildly.

This is the state Pat was in when Eileen found her late that afternoon. Eileen gently called her name, trying not to frighten her even further. "My dream terrors are worse than ever. I cannot seem to control them anymore. I am afraid, really afraid, that I will go mad," Pat explained as her whole body trembled.

June Nelson

She leaned into Eileen, who led her towards the living room. She was relieved to have someone around to help her. Eileen tried to calm her down, but holding the warm teacup in her two hands and sitting at the table, Pat was determined to talk. "Nobody could even imagine what living in Nazi-occupied Paris was like. The never-ending tension, fear, and constant looking over your shoulder, imagining every person, every sound behind you was a threat."

She was only one amongst many who had lost people who had been part of their everyday lives. She recalled the local shoemaker who was arrested in early '41, marched down the street with a gun stuck in his back, never to be seen again. She could not forget the sweet Lewinski family who lived above her with their two children. The twins were identical, and Pat could never make out whether it was vivacious, clever Eve or the gentler, more musical Rosa who knocked on her door occasionally and asked her to tell them the story of her home and family in Ireland. They would sit at her table and soak up all the funny minute details about her brothers and sisters and their lives as a large family, so incredibly different to their own. One day in late May '42, the twins called to see her. Pat could hardly contain her shock at seeing the yellow stars their mother had sewn onto their little coats in the futile hope that she could save them from the rumoured terrors that the Nazis were inflicting on Jews elsewhere. On a glorious summer day in mid-July, she last saw the Lewinski family outside her building. They were crowded aboard a Nazi truck crowded with people of all ages. The family carried small cases and waved goodbye to her.

These memories added to her feeling of loss. She was still deeply upset about Bill's murder. She knew Eileen would have great empathy for her, as she had been a nurse in London during the Second World War. They sensed that by speaking about these traumatic events, Pat would be able to cleanse herself of all her haunting memories. Time moved very slowly during these afternoon talks, and they shared much laughter and many tears. Eileen filled her notebooks with many stories, but she didn't write the stories in too much detail, as Pat spoke so quickly that she found it impossible to capture everything. For some stories, Eileen just wrote down headings, hoping to return at later stage to complete them. She had learned early on that Pat became exhausted if she let her ramble on about everything. Pat's habit of jumping from topic to topic meant that Eileen had to make quick decisions about what seemed most relevant. As Pat disliked being either interrupted or directed, Eileen often struggled to find diplomatic ways to steer the reminiscences back to individual stories. The trick was to make Pat believe it was her own idea to resume the telling of a particular incomplete story. Finally, Eileen succeeded in gently manipulating her to relate the complete story of how Bill's partner Chris had contacted her the year after the war ended.

Late one afternoon after Pat had taken her daily nap, a song came on the radio as she drank her second cup of strong, sweet tea. Pat could never get over the fact that she could now indulge in tea drinking as often as she wished—tea had been strictly rationed during the war years. She started to absentmindedly hum "La Vie en Rose" before singing the words softly. It was the most popular song in Paris in 1946, and the words held poignant memories for her.

She spoke particularly of the day she answered a knock at her door to find a tall, very thin, fair-haired man with one empty tweed jacket sleeve tucked into the pocket. Edith Piaf's words had just popped into Pat's mind: "And when you speak, angels sing from above."

Immediately, she knew from his sad expression that this had to be Bill's beloved Chris. Words seldom failed Pat, but she told Eileen that she just put her arm around Chris and without speaking, guided him to the very table they were presently seated at. There was no need for any prompting, as Pat's words flowed like tears. Chris was such a perfect captive audience for her outpouring of affection for Bill. She had described in detail her first meeting with him and how she was greatly taken by his gentleness and shocked at how damaged and ill he appeared. She described the hours-long chats they had while waiting for detailed news of the plans that the Paris Resistance were organising. She told

June Nelson

Chris about the great pleasure they had taken in their meagre meals as well as the avid attention they paid to BBC World News on the radio while sitting in the darkened room.

Chapter 36

Many Memories, Not Enough Time

Flexing her right hand to ease a cramp, Eileen put down her pen. Pat, who had not spoken for some time, was now asleep, her head tucked down on her chest, revealing the snow-white roots that had grown out from her "permanently dyed" titian hair. For the first time, Eileen noticed how old Pat had become. She had such a vibrant personality that it was impossible not to be captivated by her ageless mentality, particularly whenever she so animatedly talked through so many sad memories. Glancing up at the walnut-encased clock on top of the bookshelves, Eileen was shocked to note that three hours had passed. Pat was a fascinating storyteller once you got used to her method of skipping back and forth between stories. Eileen decided to put Pat's memories in order. She went back over her notes, dividing the pages into separate story piles, which she carefully clipped together, numbering each one as she went. Fixing the tendrils of her black hair neatly into the hairnet that covered her bun, she stretched out her legs, smoothed her navy skirt with her tired hands, and allowed herself to read back over her work.

Pat slowly awakened from her snooze, pretending that she had not been asleep. Eileen wondered if she was ever going to continue Chris's story. Shrugging her shoulders and looking Eileen straight in the eye, Pat continued. Once Pat had told Chris all about the time she and Bill had spent together, Chris began to relax. So much so that he began to relate his own memories of how his relationship with Bill had begun and developed. Their genuine mutual affection for Bill created a very warm atmosphere in the little flat. Life in the prisoner-of-war camp had been very tough for Chris. The Germans had captured him very quickly after shooting their plane down; they kept him for some time in a holding camp, where the treatment was so harsh that he was surprised he had survived. Chris's shattered left arm was already showing signs of gangrene, but luckily, a German officer allowed the medical staff to treat him. This had happened just before the prisoners were transferred to Poland. It quickly became clear to them all that they could not save the limb, so the medical team decided to operate. Once they had amputated Chris's arm, they transferred him to Poland on a cattle train. Chris and many other captives, including the diseased, ill, and contagious, were packed tightly together inside hot carriages. Pat knew from stories she had heard that Chris must have led a tortured existence in Poland. He told her that he and Bill had loved each other deeply and that he had never stopped thinking about him. Those loving thoughts were what kept him going.

Pat told Eileen how she had taken such pleasure in asking Chris to go over to her bookcase to remove a slim, black notebook from its shelves—her diary. She had always kept a diary, even if many entries had, of necessity, been cryptic during the war. To cope with the long, dark evenings, she had encouraged Bill to do the same. How wonderful to see Chris's expression as he consumed every word and little pencil sketch in Bill's diary. Some of the sketches meant nothing to Pat, but Chris was able to recognise them and tell her about the little tree with a basket underneath it where they used to escape together whenever they had rare time off. The brief diary contained all sorts of personal items that meant something only to Chris. Bill had described clouds and treetops that he could see from the flat. He had written about the hope he took from birds singing as though life were normal. At the end of the notebook, Chris found a drawing of a shamrock with a P on the top leaf, C on the right and B on the left. Initially, Pat had teased Bill, saying it was like a drawing of the Holy Trinity. However, she stopped when it became clear it was a symbol that linked the three of them together. The revelation had moved her more than she could explain.

The time they spent together turned out to be a good healing process for both of them. Pat told Chris about the many occasions when Bill spoke about him, wondering where and how he was. She had been very taken by Chris's beautiful manners and his deep respect as well as his obvious love for Bill. She told him that the fact that he had survived meant so much and hoped it made sense of a very senseless war. She was aware that Chris needed something to believe in before he could allow himself to make the best of his life without Bill. The sincerity of their love was undeniable, even if it was not what many considered the norm. Nevertheless, something deep inside Pat felt Bill wanted her to do everything in her power to convince him. That's why on the evening before Chris left, Pat insisted as only she could that he keep her most treasured possession, the shamrock Bill had made for her.

Both knew how important this little shamrock was to Pat, and that made it more special to Chris. He promised to treasure it always.

Chris spent a week with Pat. They developed a deep friendship that was to last the rest of their lives. She had no interest in what society deemed acceptable, particularly if a friendship or love was based on goodness, as had obviously been the case with Chris and Bill. Throughout her life, Pat always championed the underdog. Flitting back and forth over Chris and Bill's story and recording all of Pat's many fascinating experiences was more a pleasure than a chore for Eileen. With her meticulous storytelling detail and amusing anecdotes, Pat possessed the ability to bring people and situations to life. Eileen wrote, listed, and filed with surprising speed, and there was much laughter and endless cups of tea during these hours.

Even though Pat had been living at 8 Villa Guizot for years, she never tired of visiting the many parks and places of interest nearby. Two of her favourites were the Tomb of the Unknown Warrior and Place de l'Etoile. Pat and Eileen often went for walks there to clear their heads as well as to take a break from the little flat. Pat pointed out the places she'd mentioned in her stories. Sometimes, Eileen would squeeze her aunt's arm tightly and allow her to take a breath as sorrow overcame her.

They visited St Michael's church where Pat, at Bill's request, had lit many candles for the allied airmen she helped during the war. The smell of incense and candlewax made the two women feel as though time had stood still.

Chapter 37

Crossing the Date off the Calendar

Crossing the date off the calendar in her flat at No. 8 Villa Guizot, Pat could not have been happier. It was 2 May 1983. She had just put down the phone, having received a call from two of her many friends who were due to pick her up in an hour. They would travel by car to the south of France for a short holiday. It was to be a very special trip, as her eighty-seventh birthday was fast approaching. Her friends were treating her to a stay at a family chateau, where a few of her closest friends would get together on the Saturday evening. The chateau had a beautiful sun terrace, which overlooked a large rose garden below. Pat had been there before and loved it not only for its fairytale-like structure and many beautifully decorated rooms but also because of the incredibly lush scenery that rolled out for miles all around it. Life was perfect. There was this trip to look forward to, with all its lavish celebrations, and after that, she would travel home to spend a few days in Killeshin. Pat felt blessed.

In her little hallway, she had two sets of luggage ready—one for the south of France, the other for Ireland. The bags bulged with gifts for everyone at home. Pat had personally selected each item. Indeed, she had done so much research while at home the previous time that she was convinced the gifts would bring plenty of pleasure and joy. Along with the usual bags of clothes and books and newspaper clippings, she was especially pleased with the posters she had bought the previous week at the market in Rungis. A neighbour in Killeshin had asked her for posters for their child's school, and Pat hated to disappoint anyone, especially a young person. She valued education highly, and that the posters were destined for the local school meant a lot to her. Throughout the years, she had helped find work or educational opportunities for many young people from Ireland. Taking the posters out of their cardboard tubes, she could not help but admire the images and maps of places of interest in Paris as well as in various other regions of France. "Godfathers, I hope I don't crush them—I have so much luggage. Mon dieu, it would be a tragedy; after all, the child asked for them herself."

She took a pile of labels from the table. She had neatly written her name, address, and destination in large black letters on each label, and now she carefully tied one to each of her suitcases. Standing back, she let out a sigh of contentment and then went to make herself a quick cup of tea before she left. Sitting in her favourite chair with the long net curtains billowing in the breeze that only a warm Paris afternoon can bring, she watched as a shard of light played across the old bookcase. There were no books on those shelves anymore; Pat had moved them to a newer, larger bookcase across the room a few years before. She felt as though she had not seen the photos and mementoes on the shelf for a long time. A combination of photographs of beloved people mostly gone now and the sound of the forlorn accordion below playing "La Vie en Rose", the tune drifting gently upwards, made her nostalgic. She went through each of the names in the photographs, speaking them out loud in a type of homage. Then, when the sound of the doorbell interrupted her, she whispered, "Poppycock!" She stood upright, keeping her back stiff and her nose in the air, and straightened her tweed skirt. Then she left her flat for the very last time.

"Bonjour, bonjour, c'est si excitant," Pat gushed as she sat into the front seat of the car, leaving Paul, her red-faced friend and driver, to put her heavy bags into an already overcrowded boot.

It was a very busy afternoon in Paris, and the traffic was manic. Car horns blared from every side street, trying to attract attention as they sought permission to head towards one of the many exits out of the city. The route to the south of France was especially congested. Pat could not help but feel a little apprehensive. Her gut told her that something was not quite right, and she could not understand why. A beautiful day, an amazing trip ahead, and yet… There was something off. They finally made their way to the main road towards the south, Pat started to relax. She was just speaking to Paul when she saw it approaching—a large white truck swinging across the road in their direction. She saw the truck driver's face, saw him mouth "Merde!" Everything went into slow motion. She heard the screeching of the rubber tyres as Paul tried to avoid the impact, and they headed towards a large tree at the side of the road. She heard screaming. It sounded as if it was in the distance. She realised her mouth was wide open and that it was her scream. Then she saw flecks of dust, white in the sunlight, floating all around her as though dancing to a very slow tune. A noise of scrunched metal. Time was suspended. The light was silver now, and as her eyes adjusted and her body pitched forward towards the windscreen, she could see her younger self, aged about four years, turning towards her and with a gentle smile, waving before changing into herself aged twenty or so in her flapper dress, defiantly smoking her cigarette. Then herself at the same age playing tennis in Villa Durenne, and later still, there she was holding the green dragon lighter in Café Jacque in 1941. Finally, they came—images of Mother, Father, Christine, Paddy, Gertie, Scholastica, John, Kitty, and even little Vera.

Stretching out her gnarled hand, she joined them.

Epilogue

The Grave in Killeshin

It happens to us all one time or another. That warm, strange feeling that we are in the right place at the right time. People speak about stars aligning, but I think it is fate, just fate. Last summer, we made a journey to Kilkenny. We turned off the motorway early, deciding to visit the lovely village of Castlecomer. We drove along familiar, small, bendy local roads before arriving at the Glenside Pub where Aunt Pat was born.

Behind the pub at the top of a very steep hill lies Killeshin Church, a place I am very familiar with. It was a warm, sunny August day with a gentle breeze whispering around us— a perfect day to visit the family graves.

I stood looking at Aunt Pat's simple grave, and I felt deeply moved. Touching the headstone, I said out loud, "Aunt Pat, I have done it. I have finished the book."

I felt at peace then. All around me were people who had loved me as I had loved them. As I write this, I feel emotional about the experience. It has meant so much to me to go on a journey that taught me so much about endurance and strength, as well as finally just bloody finishing something.

June Nelson

Printed in Great Britain
by Amazon